Ghost Trancer
A Hypnotist Among the Spirits

Ghost Trancer
A Hypnotist Among the Spirits

Michael
Mezmer

FAYETTEVILLE
MAFIA
PRESS

Cover by Michael Mezmer
All photos by Linda "Susie" Davis
Edited by David Bushman
Book design by Scott Ryan

Published in the USA by Fayetteville Mafia Press
Columbus, Ohio

Contact Information
Email: fayettevillemafiapress@gmail.com
Website: fayettevillemafiapress.com
Instagram: @fayettevillemafiapress
Twitter:@Fmpbooks

ISBN: 9781949024463
eBook ISBN: 9781949024470

"There are more things in heaven and earth, Horatio,
Than are dreamt of in your philosophy."

Shakespeare
Hamlet Act 1 Scene 5

CONTENTS

Foreword by Don Smeraldi..*viii*

1. Beginnings..*1*

2. The Coal Miner's Angel...*9*

3. The Screaming Woman in Cabin 606.......................................*17*

4. What Haunts in Vegas Curses in Vegas..................................*31*

5. The Ghost of Walt Disney..*37*

6. The Cry of the Donkey Lady and Other Haunts of Old
      San Antonio..*42*

7. Prisoners of the Spirit World...*53*

8. The Dead of Deadwood..*63*

9. Ghosts of the Nevada Desert...................................73

10. The Tell-Tale Heart of the Clark Chateau..................*81*

11. Invitation to a Ghost Town.................................*88*

12. Call of the Voodoo Drums...................................*97*

13. Not Goodbye, Only So Long.................................*104*

Acknowledgments...*108*

About the Author..*110*

More to Read..*112*

—FOREWORD—

They say talent comes in all shapes and sizes, but when it comes to Michael Mezmer, he's one size fits all. As a magazine publisher and forty-year communications professional, I have never known a more multitalented, passionate, and sincere person so dedicated to his craft, his family, and those he has helped clinically in a medical setting and entertained at his shows worldwide.

Vicki—my wife and co-publisher of *Scary Monsters* magazine— and I first came to know Michael through his skillful and illustrious writing about the intersection of hypnosis and magic in classic horror and sci-fi movies. His unique perspective, formulated over many years as a clinical hypnotherapist and professional magician, has provided our readers new and interesting ways to enjoy and examine films they know and love as well as ones they may have not been familiar with but have learned to appreciate. This has been recognized by Michael being named a runner-up for Writer of the Year for 2017 in the Seventeenth Annual Rondo Hatton Classic Horror Awards. He also has contributed significantly to *Scary Monsters* being voted Best Classic Horror Magazine in the Rondo Awards for the past five years in a row (2017–2021). In addition, his enthusiastic appearances on radio programs and podcasts have helped publicize both the magazine and the classic movie genres embraced by "Monster Kids" around the globe.

Michael's article "Hypnosis and Monsters: Beware the Hypnotic Eye" in *Scary Monsters* Issue 110 explained how hypnosis had been incorporated into such early films as *The Cabinet of Dr. Caligari* (1920), *Svengali* (1931), and *The She-Creature* (1956) and on television in the original *Dark Shadows* (1966-1971). He went on to write in detail about some of the hypnosis techniques and magic tricks showcased in fan favorite *The Hypnotic Eye* (1960). In Issue 113, he told the story of his levitation demonstration in 1973 of the late actress Jeanne Bates, whose career included roles in the feature films *The Return of the Vampire* (1943), *The Soul of a Monster* (1944), and *The Mask of Diijon* (1946) and such television shows as *Alcoa Presents: One Step Beyond* (1959-1961) and *The Twilight Zone* (1959-1964). In his article "The Monster in the Closet Meets the Man of a Thousand Faces" for Issue 116, he shared his interest and talents in monster movie makeup and cosplay, performed alongside his daughter, Ilia.

Most recently, Michael was voted a runner-up for Best Article in the Rondo Awards for 2021 for the two-parter "Of Monsters and Magic" in Issues 121 and 122. A year earlier, he had introduced our readers to his highly developed ghost-hunting skills and real-life adventures, including all the amazing investigative tools, in "Monster Kid-Ghost Hunter: Fantasy vs. Reality!" published in Issue 118. This fascinating foray into the ghostly and supernatural realms led to Issue 123 and the magazine's in-depth coverage of Ed and Lorraine Warren and the Conjuring Universe. His article also inspired me to go on my own ghost-hunting experience.

While Michael takes the paranormal activities he has encountered over the years very seriously, he explains each situation in an understandable and entertaining way. Prepare yourself as Michael Mezmer takes you on an amazing journey of scary discovery.

Don Smeraldi
Publisher/Editor
Scary Monsters **and** ***Castle of Frankenstein*** **magazines**

—CHAPTER 1—

Beginnings

I have traveled throughout the US and abroad in search of the unknown. From Indonesia to the Caribbean and to the Rocky Mountains, I have seen and experienced things most people see only in fictional films and written stories--ancient trance ceremonies in Thailand, headhunters in Indonesia, and many unbelievable things in between. In this book I will be telling the stories of some of my real-life ghost-hunting experiences, many of which I have never discussed before. Everything you are about to read actually happened to me with the exception of the stories I share about my grandfather (Grandpap), whose experiences happened before I was born, when he was a coal miner. Almost every investigation and supernatural phenomenon associated with those investigations were viewed by one or more witnesses, and most were documented on video and in photos.

We will journey together to a haunted chateau, an antiquated prison, Las Vegas casinos, legendary haunted bridges, authentic Old West ghost towns, and many more locales, including several countries abroad. We'll encounter ghosts, poltergeists, and a legendary cryptid.

A question I am often asked is "How does one become a ghost hunter?" There is no one single answer. There are no traditional colleges that offer training or degrees on investigating the spirit world. Some paranormal experts have apprentices who eventually move on to their own investigations. A person driven to ghost hunt has more than likely had an interest in the spirit world for a very long time. Some people are born with natural special abilities—a sixth sense—affording them a head start. Others have no noticeable special abilities but have always felt an inner need to explore the spirit realm. Others still are simply fascinated by ghosts, so pursue the field as a hobby. The more people we have investigating, the more evidence can be gathered and examined, and the better it is for paranormal investigation.

In my case, I was attracted to the world of movie monsters and magic at a very young age. Movies about ghosts and creatures comforted me as a child. Because my parents were older and were bothered by kids making noise, and also possibly breaking valued collectibles, friends rarely visited me at home. As a result, monsters were my "friends." I have always been fascinated by Halloween. Most kids looked forward to Christmas presents under the tree; I was sad that Halloween was ten months away. I have been an outsider my entire life.

As a small child, I was drawn to cemeteries and graveyards. When my parents and I would drive back East to visit relatives in Ohio, I would ask my dad to stop whenever I spotted an old cemetery or graveyard along the way so that I could take photos of the tombstones and create picture albums. Never have I sensed negative energy in these places; rather, I feel at peace—comforted on a deep level. I have always been a night person. That too aids me in ghost hunting.

I probably should mention—since we will be using these terms throughout the book —that there is a specific difference between cemeteries and graveyards. A cemetery is a burial ground unattached to a church; a graveyard, on the other hand, is located on church grounds.

At what age did I make the jump from the fantasy world of ghost stories and monster movies to actually seeking contact with the dead? As I wrote this book, that question began to "haunt" me. As a magician and illusionist who has toured the world with my TranceNosis comedy hypnosis and DangerMagik magic phenomena shows, I have created the theatrical illusion of a connection to the spirit realm many times, but how did I make the leap of faith to one step beyond? In pondering this question, I realized that during my childhood, I was exposed to many stories of the paranormal —some fictional, some not.

In researching, writing, and reliving the stories I include here, I ultimately realized that all of my life I have possessed a strange, somewhat supernatural ability to sense a variety of things, primarily about family members, or sometimes close friends—not like mentalists or mind readers who can predict the future on demand or tell you what color your underclothes are. Rather, it's an organic, inner, somewhat unfocused ability that allows me to sense certain feelings of those closest to me. The Bible calls it the "power of discernment"; in the paranormal world, it is called ESP, or extrasensory perception. I believe I may have inherited this ability from Grandpap, whom you will learn about in the next chapter. I now believe this special ability may have drawn me to the spirit realm.

On the fantasy side of the equation, many TV shows influenced my young mind. What kid of the fifties and sixties can forget the lovable Casper the Friendly Ghost? Casper first appeared in animated form in 1945, and starting 1963 his cartoon adventures were syndicated throughout the country on television. In 1995, he was the virtual character in a feature film—the first to make extended use of computer-generated imagery. For me, a lonely last child of three, with brothers who were ten and twenty years older, Casper was another imaginary friend. I still have the Casper talking stuffed doll that I took to bed with me every night as a child. In looking back, I suspect Casper softened my young mind to the concept of the spirit world, convincing me it was a friendly place.

In the late sixties, reruns of the live-action sitcom *Topper* (1953-1955) also influenced me. Based on the 1937 film of the same name, the show starred Anne Jeffreys, Robert Sterling, and Leo G. Carroll, later Alexander Waverly of *The Man from U.N.C.L.E.* The plot involved a haunted house and a husband-and-wife ghost team and ghost dog who wreaked havoc on poor Cosmo Topper (Carroll)—more fun inside the ghostly realms. As I moved into my preteen years, I fell under the sway of the legendary supernatural daytime soap opera *Dark Shadows*, in particular the story of Quentin Collins. Watching Quentin's ghost silently brood as he manipulated two young children was, in one sense, unsettling, yet simultaneously intriguing. (On a side note, I was lucky enough to spend an entire day in 1970 on the set of the original *Dark Shadows*—as opposed to the 1991 remake—and it was wonderful meeting all my heroes from the cast and watching them work.)

Looking back, I can see that all of these pop culture artifacts had a great impact on my young, formative mind, opening up my imagination to the possibilities of life after death.

However, I didn't begin ghost hunting in earnest until I was an adult, especially over the past decade. Until then, I suppose, I feared that being associated with searching for ghosts might have a negative impact on my career: if I revealed my interest in the supernatural and made the jump to actually exploring the spirit world, my thinking went, people might look at me askance. Then, at some point, I finally began to realize that ghost hunting had become acceptable to the general public and, in fact, was actually considered a pretty cool thing to do.

Pioneers like Hanz Holzer (an Austrian-American author and parapsychologist who wrote numerous books on the supernatural and had his own *Ghost Hunter* TV series) and Peter James (most well-known for his extensive paranormal investigations of the Queen Mary) had a major impact on the public's willingness to embrace the plausibility of ghosts. As a point of personal history, Hanz and I were both guests on a local LA-area TV show in the 1970s. He was a fascinating person.

It was not until the modern era, particularly the past decade or so, that ghost hunting was no longer frowned upon as eccentric or bizarre behavior. Many reality series feature paranormal themes. Two of the most prominent are the Travel Channel's *The Dead Files*, starring Amy Allan and Steve DiSchiavi, and *Ghost Adventures*, starring the charismatic Zak Bagans. These shows have brought ghost hunting into the mainstream. I came to realize that hunting ghosts would not only be fascinating, but also enhance my career as a magician and hypnotist, thus freeing me to follow a path that somehow I had always known was part of my destiny. Paranormal investigating would add to my mystique, not unlike Houdini, who in the latter part of his career became well-known for his investigations of the spirit world.

At that point, I began to familiarize myself with the tools of the trade, to enhance my investigations. Modern ghost hunters use a variety of devices to sense the presence of spirits. One of our most common tools is the EMF meter, used to measure electromagnetic fields. Most of these meters measure the electromagnetic radiation flux density (DC fields) or the change in an electromagnetic field over time (AC fields), essentially the same as a radio antenna but with quite different detection characteristics. For whatever reasons, spirits seem to be drawn to localized electromagnetic fields. When on a ghost hunt, we make sure if possible that all of the electricity is turned off at that location before we begin, to facilitate accurate responses.

The presence of spirits also triggers extreme drops in temperature. Therefore, another effective tool is a temperature gun, an infrared thermometer combined with a laser, which measures temperature from a distance. Standard handheld digital recorders can capture electronic voice phenomena, or EVP, because they can pick up sounds typically undetected by the human ear, as discovered during playback.

Another useful tool is a spirit box of some sort; my personal preference is the Sono X ghost box, an app I've downloaded onto my iPad. The device rotates a bank of random words and phrases; when spirits wish to communicate, they seem to be able to manipulate the words and phrases that are stored in the app into meaningful spoken phrases to make their presence known. One thing to keep in mind, given what you're about to read: personal information, like names, is not included in the bank.

My favorite tools of the trade include classic dowsing rods, which are extremely sensitive to spirit activity; standard flashlights, effective for conducting question-and-answer sessions with the other side; and parabolic microphones, allowing the investigator to hear and record subtle, distant sounds of paranormal activity that normally are beyond the range of the human ear.

Of course, many more sophisticated tools and phone apps are available, but in all honesty, these basic tools can be the most effective, and are what most hunters work with.

Another question people usually ask me is "Do you believe ghosts are real?"

Of course my answer is yes.

Then people ask, "What do you believe ghosts are?"

I can answer that question only from my own point of view, based on what I have seen and experienced. Grandpap might have interpreted ghosts as angels; for me, they are simply the spirits of those who have passed away and have a need to communicate with us or seek help in moving on.

Another question often posed to ghost hunters: "Are spirits demonic, violent, or malevolent?"

We've all seen so many films and TV shows in which spirits are evil and harmful to living humans. It's important to understand that this type of entertainment (including reality shows) is just that— entertainment—and that good drama makes for good television and film.

The Others, a 2001 psychological horror film starring Nicole Kidman, best explains my theory of the spirit realm. Written, directed, and scored by Alejandro Amenábar, the film takes place in 1945; Grace Stewart (Kidman) occupies a remote country house in the fog-encased countryside of Jersey, a Channel Island, along with her two young children, Anne and Nicholas. Throughout the film, they seem to be haunted by various specters. At the end of the film (SPOILER ALERT!), we discover that the Stewarts aren't being haunted at all, but rather, unbeknown to them, are themselves the ghosts, haunting the current residents of the house.

Personally, I have never found ghosts to be harmful or evil. I think they often have unfinished business to attend to, which explains their continued presence in this realm. I truly believe spirits, like those in the movie, simply do not realize they are no longer alive, and at certain places and times somehow intersect with our reality. That is when communication between their world and ours happens. This, I postulate, is why we can communicate with them one minute through a device like the ghost box, only for the veil to close the next.

People also often ask me, "Do you ever get scared or frightened during investigations?"

My answer is no; I have always felt at home with the spirit world. Respecting the spirits you encounter is vital when trying to make contact. The very first thing I do when arriving at a supposedly haunted location is say a prayer of protection. I then make it clear to whomever may be listening that I am there to help them in whatever way I can. I never raise my voice or challenge spirits adversarially.

Kindness goes a long way with ghosts.

When I depart an investigation site, I make sure the spirits know I'm leaving, and if I'm unable to help them move on, I volunteer that they must stay at their home and I must go to mine. I always make a point of thanking them for the visit.

I should mention that my approach to ghost hunting is unique, as I have an extremely specialized skill set. I'm an award-winning magician, clinical hypnotherapist, and stage hypnotist. Harry Houdini famously debunked spiritualists through his knowledge of magic. I do want to make it clear that while I am hardly a skeptic, I'm also not completely a true believer in all aspects of the supernatural. And yet, I want to believe.

I can state with absolute certainty that after having experienced firsthand the stories you are about to read, I have reached the point where I know something is happening beyond normal human experience. But just what that something is, I'm still searching out. Not unlike Fox Mulder in *The X-Files*, I believe "The truth is out there." And like Houdini before me, I am, as an extremely skilled magician, able to analyze the supernatural phenomena that I experience during an investigation and deduce whether it is, in fact, valid. As a hypnotist, I can apply my skills and knowledge to enhance my communication techniques in interacting with the spirit realm. By holding hypnotherapy sessions with those who have themselves undergone supernatural experiences, I can help them better understand and cope with whatever it is they encountered.

As I dig deeper into ghost hunting, the more I notice that many others among us boast unusual skill sets of their own. For instance, a gentleman named Joshua Bartholomew with Bozeman Paranormal Society, based in Montana, is deaf; thus, his other senses are heightened, empowering him to detect things beyond the capabilities of other investigators. Another investigator I know possesses a beautiful voice and communicates with spirits by singing to them. The possibilities are endless.

One thing I will say unequivocally is that investigating paranormal activity can lead to exhilarating adventure. I never know what will transpire from one haunted location to the next. The rewards are bountiful—maybe not from a financial aspect, but in helping lost souls, and sometimes troubled souls, find peace in the afterlife. In a way, ghost hunting is just another form of time travel, as you find yourself communicating with spirits who lived long in the past, sometimes hundreds of years earlier.

One word of caution before you read on: *real* ghost hunting is nothing like what you see in *Ghostbusters* or even many paranormal reality shows. Perhaps "hunting" is even a misnomer of sorts. We're not looking to capture or expose ghosts; we're simply looking to make contact and help ease their way into the afterlife, should they choose to do so, by settling any unpaid debts left here in the material world. I see myself merely as a guest in the spirits' space, and my goal is to be respectful, to never agitate or upset them. It's a constant balancing act, weighing intellectual curiosity against the need to respect the rights of the spirit. If, in the following pages, it appears that I am departing an investigation at just the wrong time, or recoiling in fear, rest assured that what I am actually doing is honoring the boundaries of the spirit world.

I want to thank you for reading my book, and invite you to sit back in your easy chair and join me on this journey into a strange new world, where the supernatural becomes the natural and the paranormal becomes the normal.

I encourage you to set aside any skepticism you may have; open your mind and your imagination as I share with you some of the most incredible stories of my life.

—CHAPTER 2—
The Coal Miner's Angel

In many ways, we are shaped by our past and by the family members who have come before us. In my extensive study as a clinical hypnotherapist and while earning a degree in psychology from California Coast University, I have learned that for the first seven years of our lives, we typically uncritically accept information given to us by those we look up to or perceive as authority figures. After that, we begin to develop a "critical factor," enabling us to filter out whatever information we choose to independently reject or accept.

I was fortunate enough to have some very good role models in my young life. One of the finest people I have ever known was not an educated man; nor was he rich or a great leader of men. Still, he was inspirational to me in so many crucial ways. My grandpa on my Dad's side, or, as we called him, Grandpap, was a coal miner in West Virginia—a simple, hardworking man who often told me his life was much like the Tennessee Ernie Ford song "Sixteen Tons," written by Merle Travis. For those unfamiliar with the song, here are a few of the lyrics:

> You load 16 tons, what do you get?
> Another day older and deeper in debt
> Saint Peter, don't you call me, 'cause I can't go
> I owe my soul to the company store.

My Grandpap, a coal miner for fifty-five years, literally lived the life outlined in that song. Amazingly, he never contracted black lung, and he lived a long life—long enough to retire and, in the process, buy property on a hillside overlooking the Ohio River, where he built houses for not just himself, but also most of his children and their families. Think Walton Mountain in TV's *The Waltons*.

But how does Grandpap connect to ghosts and the spirit realm? First and foremost, he was deeply spiritual. As a young man, I was impressed by his knowledge of the Bible and his ability, it seemed, to converse with angels. Often we would be playing or sitting together, and in the middle of a discussion he would stop and listen to some otherworldly voice that only he could hear.

"Thank you, Lord," he would reply.

Christians call this the "power of discernment." I assure you Grandpap wasn't mentally askew in any way—in fact, quite the opposite. He was extremely present and sharp, and worked on cars almost to the age of ninety. I mention this because it sets the framework for three supernatural experiences Grandpap lived through and related to me when I was a young boy; I accepted them uncritically, and they have catalyzed my work as an investigator of the spirit world.

***

When Grandpap was a young man, his dream was to play professional baseball, and he was even scouted by the Pittsburgh Pirates. Unfortunately, Grandpap had short, stubby thumbs, so even though he was a talented player, he couldn't throw a good fastball. This crushed his dream, forcing him to follow another path in life.

At the time, Grandpap lived just across the river from Wheeling, West Virginia, where most young men wound up becoming factory workers or coal miners—or working for the mob. Grandpap chose the mines.

Imagine toiling away for hours and hours in a cold, damp coal mine, outfitted in a helmet with a T-shaped leather lamp bracket with a carbide lamp attached at the front—a beacon of light in the blackness of the claustrophobic cave. The interior of the helmet consisted of a leather headband connected to eight suspension straps; I still have one in my home today, and treasure it. His other tools included picks, shovels, and —perhaps most importantly—a mule. Health and safety rules were virtually nonexistent; many good men perished way before their time from lung disease.

A man of faith, Grandpap never felt alone in the mine. He knew in his heart that God was there alongside him every minute of every day.

One cold winter day, Grandpap left the company housing and trudged across the snow-covered trail into the darkness of the predawn morning. He always carried a canary in a cage with him into the mine, to warn him if there was an issue with oxygen. He also carried a lunch box, which typically included a warm pastie.

At first, this particular morning seemed no different from any other day. As Grandpap swung his pick, the muscles in his back tensed all the way to the base of his spine. Then, as he began to take another swing, the blackness of the cavern was suddenly bathed in white light, so much so that Grandpap had to shield his eyes from the blinding brightness. Finally able to focus his eyes, he saw something that would change his life forever.

Standing before him, all aglow, was an angel.

"Leave the mine immediately, " the celestial harbinger told him.

Understand that in these times, coal miners were almost literally owned by the company they worked for; leaving in the middle of a shift was strictly prohibited. The rule was you filled your quota no matter what. But seeing the angel and hearing its message, Grandpap knew he had to leave, and quickly.

He didn't, however, know why. He wondered if there might be something wrong at home with his wife. After leaving the mine with little explanation, he made his way home, where he found that Grandma was just fine. After sharing a cup of coffee with Grandma, he decided to turn around and head back to the mine. He trusted that his vision of the angel was real, but he also knew he'd be expected to return to work.

Upon returning to work, he was devastated by what he encountered:. the mine had collapsed, and all of the other men on his shift had perished. They were laid out on the ground, and as wives began arriving to claim their husband's bodies, they howled in anguish.

Unsurprisingly, this incident had a major impact on Grandpap, strengthening his faith even more. I know Grandpap always regretted that he hadn't advised the other miners to leave the mine, but he hadn't even entertained the possibility that he was the one in danger rather than Grandma.

Who was the harbinger of this warning? From Grandpap's point of view, it was an angel, but depending on your orientation, it could have been a ghost or spirit. Or perhaps they are all one in the same? In any case, it was a supernatural being that, for whatever reason, was sent to save my Grandpap's life.

As far as I was concerned, Grandpap always told the truth. He had no reason to invent that story. And my grandma backed it up. As a young man hearing this story for the first time, I was convinced that there was much more to life and to our world than the eye can see. We are never alone. Grandpap's story was comforting and mysterious at the same time.

And this was not the only story involving the spirit realm that Grandpap shared with me. He was a good man, but he did have a weakness—one that would unfortunately pass down to my father. Grandpap loved to gamble. I will never understand why. His salary from the mines wasn't much, and yet still he was gripped by a compulsion to gamble away some of that hard-earned pay.

Understand when I say gambling, I don't mean at a legal casino. The mob ran most of the gambling houses in Wheeling. On one particular Friday night after work, he told me, he decided to head into town to gamble instead of going straight home. He had won a hefty pile of money the week before, and hoped his good fortune would continue. Still, a sense of uneasiness tugged at him.

To enter the casino, you had to go down an alley and through a back entrance. Wheeling was a rough town, but the gambling establishments and the surrounding area were protected by the mob, so safety was nothing to worry about. Yet Grandpap could not shake his feeling of dread. With each step he took toward the entrance to the gambling hall, his pace slowed. *Turn around*, a part of him warned. But the drive to gamble was too strong.

This was a time in his life that Grandpap's faith was growing even stronger, and perhaps deep down he knew what he was doing was wrong. Grandma had always pleaded with him not to gamble, knowing how tight money was, yet still, he felt compelled to do it.

Just a few feet from the door, Grandpap stopped in his tracks to reconsider the consequences of his actions for his family. As he reached for the door handle, this same sense of foreboding nagged at him. Suddenly, something felt wrong: the handle of the door was on fire! Grandpap's hand literally burned. He ran down the alley and into the night. Looking down at his hand, he could see that the burns were far more extensive than he had imagined. As quickly as he could, Grandpap returned home, and Grandma treated the hand with butter.

Grandma wondered what happened, and Grandpap explained everything. Both sat in silence, shocked and in wonder. Grandpap told me it was a message from God, advising him to never gamble again. And from that day forward, he never did.

These two stories alone confirmed for me that Grandpap was sensitive to the spirit world. But there is one more story that would have shattered any doubts I had. This was, in the truest sense of the term, a ghost story.

As I mentioned earlier, Grandpap built houses for the entire family on his hill. It was an amazing achievement for a person of limited finances. He literally built each house himself. The hill was located in Bridgeport, Ohio, just across the river from Wheeling. All of my aunts and uncles on my dad's side lived on that hill, along with all of their children. Grandpap's first wife, my Grandma, left him at one point, and he remarried. Grandpap even built a home on the hill for his new wife's sister, Cora. By the time I was old enough to know, Great-Aunt Cora's house looked very much like Norman Bates's abode in Alfred Hitchcock's *Psycho*. It was a two-story construction, weathered by the time I saw it, as a young child. The interior was also similar to the Bates home, with a stairway lurking just inside the front door.

Cora herself resembled Norman's mother. Her hair was gray and piled into a bun atop her head. She wore the same old-fashioned dresses.

I never liked visiting that house. I felt a strange, dark energy radiating from it. I didn't know how to express those feelings to my mom or my dad.

What I did not know until later in my life was that my dad's sister Thelma had fallen down the stairs of that home to her death. Eventually Great-Aunt Cora passed away, but through the years that followed, members of the family, including Grandpap, reported seeing her looking out the windows of the house. I too remember seeing Great-Aunt Cora's pale-gray apparition in the windows, staring off into the moonlight.

The incident occurred when my parents and I were visiting during Christmas time. It was a snowy and gloomy day—the ground was patched with ice. I had been at Aunt Dorothy's house, located at the top of the hill, and was heading down to see my cousin Brenda. It was dusk; the dark of night was quickly approaching. As I neared Cora's house, I slipped on the ice, but being a kid, I quickly got back on my feet. Just as I found my footing, I glanced up at Cora's house. There she stood in the upstairs bedroom window, staring hauntingly off at the emerging moonlight, clearly a full-body apparition (although I didn't know what that was back then).

For a brief moment, I was in shock, not knowing what to do. Then I hurried down the hill, gripped by fear. "Do not look behind you," the angels warned Lot, his wife, and their daughter as they fled Sodom and Gomorrah. I turned my back on Aunt Cora and the house, and never looked back.

When finally I reached Brenda's, I shared what had happened. No one expressed surprise, but simply accepted my experience as commonplace. I have to wonder if Cora was simply comforting her little great-nephew as he slipped and fell on the ice that night.

One more supernatural occurrence happened on the family hill, but of a very different kind.

Behind the homes on the hill was a densely wooded area, which included an outhouse. By the time I came into the picture, the outhouse was no longer in use, but it still stood intact, overrun with foliage. Most of my cousins would venture into the woods for adventure; my relatives on the hill were very poor, and the woods were their version of Disneyland. There was also a gorge, wide and deep, and someone had tied a rope to a tree limb so they could swing over the gorge for kicks.

One year, I spent my summer vacation with my parents in Bridgeport. It was a warm and humid night. My cousins all knew they should never be in the woods after dusk. For one thing, wildlife lived there, some of it less than friendly. For another, strangers were known to roam these woods, also sometimes less than hospitable.

On this particular night, the sun had almost set when my Aunt Virginia suddenly realized that her daughters had yet to return from the woods. I could see my aunt was getting worried, especially because my cousins Brenda and Dodo (short for Dorothy) were by themselves. Time passed, and the sky turned from gray to black. Still, no sight of my cousins. Suddenly, we heard distant screams emanating from the woods, followed by the rustling of bushes. Out of nowhere, my two cousins burst through the front door, breathing hard, sweat dripping down their faces.

"Lock the door!" they told my aunt. "Lock all the windows!"

From off in the distance, we began to hear a low, growling sound, but not one of us could identify it as belonging to animals known to live in those woods.

My cousins shook uncontrollably. When they were finally calm enough to speak rationally, they related to us their experience, all while the growling continued, seemingly getting closer and closer.

They had been walking home through the woods, and as they approached the old outhouse, they noticed that someone—or something—was inside it. That's when they first heard the growling. Suddenly, the door of the outhouse burst open, and they did the only thing they could think of to do: they ran. They claimed to have caught a brief look at the creature as it chased them, and described it as furry and foul smelling, huge and bearing the fangs of a wolf.

The field of cryptozoology was created in 1955, but in the early sixties the term "cryptid" was still largely outside public consciousness. Could it have been a cryptid of some kind that was chasing them? One of the first, and by far the best known, cryptids allegedly sited in West Virginia was known as the Grafton Monster, or Beast of Grafton. Its sighting took place on June 16, 1964, the same year my cousins were terrified in the woods. The Grafton Monster was said to be white, seven to nine feet tall and four feet wide, with seal-like skin. Although my cousins never saw the creature again, the howling in the woods continued for many months. For as long as I live, I'll remember the terrified looks on my cousins' faces as they frantically ran through the door.

I will always remember Grandpap. He was a remarkable man in so many ways and an inspiration to all the people who knew him. I feel that in some small way, I have inherited his sensitivity to the spirit world. As my Grandpap grew older, his power of discernment, and his ability to communicate with the angels, became stronger and more frequent. It seems that the veil between the world of the living and the spirit realm thins as we age. I can only hope that I will one day have the clarity that Grandpap had—he literally had no fear of crossing over, knowing it was simply a transition to a better place.

—CHAPTER 3—

The Screaming Woman in Cabin 606

Long before I became a ghost hunter in earnest, I was touched by the supernatural. As I mentioned in chapter two, my grandfather was an extremely spiritual person, in constant contact with the unseen. At this point in my life, I have to believe his special relationship with the beyond skipped a generation before being passed down to me; my father never seemed drawn to the other world. But as I grew to adulthood, the spirit world came knocking—whether I was on land or on sea, whether I was not intentionally seeking it out or not (and I mostly wasn't).

In the 1980s, I was performing my illusion show on major cruise ships around the world. For the passengers, cruise ships are a fantasy world where they feel like pampered royalty and are ferried to exotic locations that most people only dream about. The flip side of the story is that for those who live and work on these ships, it is a psychologically challenging and extremely confining life, in that you are figuratively institutionalized for months at a time, separated from everyone and everything you love and care about.

British Judge Brenda Hale once said, "A gilded cage is still a cage." On cruise ships, entertainers appear to live in luxury but actually enjoy very little freedom and very little privacy—just some limited hours on shore or in the small confines of their stateroom, but even there, the walls have ears. Many entertainers turn to alcoholism and drug abuse or become addicted to gambling; some even end their lives through suicide. Of course, this is never publicized; rather, the fate of these cruise ship entertainers is "lost at sea."

Truth is, there's a very dark side to cruising. Murders, suicides, unexplained deaths—all have been known to happen aboard cruise ships. Passengers overindulge in alcohol and illegal drugs, purchased in foreign ports. They "fall in love" with ship employees or fellow passengers in doomed relationships consummated by meaningless sex.

It's this dark side of cruising from where powerful spirit energy emerges. Some apparitions that haunt these ships are passive, but others can be violent and aggressive. Many stories have been told over the years of ghosts at sea, even of so-called ghost ships. I had always believed these stories were merely fictional tales passed from ship to ship, crew to crew, and sailor to sailor. However, my beliefs would soon be shattered.

Perhaps the spirits of those who died on ships were, like the crew members themselves, trapped aboard these hellish vessels, or perhaps they had made the choice never to leave the venue of the happiest moments of their lives.

By the time this particular incident unfolded, I had performed for several years on cruise ships originating from ports in the States and was well-adjusted to life at sea. Unlike some of my fellow entertainers and crew members, I had developed methods of enduring cruise life, so I was extremely excited to be booked as an entertainer on the *Pearl of Scandinavia*. The *Pearl* was an exclusive ship based out of Asia, with home ports in Singapore and Hong Kong. Many dignitaries and other upper-crust people sailed aboard her. Prior to being refitted as a cruise ship, she was a cargo vessel—an icebreaker that had spent extensive time at sea. No doubt she had witnessed many strange incidents over the years.

I expected my time on the *Pearl* to be a great adventure, as it had long been a dream of mine to visit the Orient. The *Pearl* had visited ports in Indonesia, the Philippines, China, Thailand, South Korea, and Japan, among others. ABC's *The Love Boat* even filmed a two-part episode aboard her.

Most of the passengers were older, experienced travelers, more interested in full-day and even overnight excursions in exotic ports rather than late-night partying on the ship. On nights before the ship docked at a port, most passengers would retire to their cabins early, leaving the public spaces nearly empty—perfectly inviting for spirits to manifest and fill.

Most passengers are not aware that death is a constant companion on cruise ships. Most vessels keep one of their meat freezers empty, or at least partially empty, to store and preserve the bodies of anyone who dies during the cruise. Some of these unfortunate souls are having the time of their lives when they pass; others are in the grip of devastating sadness. Either of these extremes, I would learn, can be an emotional anchor to the ship for their spirits. I can remember waking up several times before the passengers when we would dock early in the morning, looking out my stateroom's porthole, and seeing the black body bags being taken off the ship. The illusion of fun and happiness had to be maintained at all costs, so the bodies had to be moved when the passengers were still in dreamland. It was a morbid sight that, for me at least, evoked an Edgar Allan Poe story.

One day while sitting in the crew's bar, my fellow employees started sharing with me stories about strange happenings they had witnessed or experienced—always taking place very early in the morning, when the passengers were asleep. Crew bars on cruise ships have a radically different atmosphere than the lavish public spaces just a few decks above; typically, they're poorly lit and sparsely decorated. Like at any bar, the patrons would loosen their lips and share their most guarded thoughts after tossing a few shots down the hatch. There'd be a lot of joking, but when crew members shared stories about supernatural experiences on board, they were deadly serious. It was as if by sharing their stories, they could purge the nightmares that haunted them. I think that is why I started to believe them. Many times I saw abject fear reflected in their eyes.

The senior officers on board the ship were Danish, mostly very staunch and proper, so ghost stories never came from them. But other members of the crew were Filipinos who were devout Catholics. Prior to the arrival of Spanish missionaries, Filipinos practiced many different indigenous religions that embraced multiple gods and unique concepts of the soul. Many members of the crew still clung to these beliefs, which, I think, opened their hearts and minds to the spirit energies around them.

I recall a conversation late one night in the crew bar while I was visiting with several of the Filipino female dancers from the entertainment department. Evelyn was the lead dancer, a bit older than the others. On most nights she preferred socializing with her own group, but on this particular night she asked me, "Do you believe in ghosts?"

Quickly, I replied, " Yes."

"Many times the other girls and I have woken up and see an old lady dressed in white sitting at the foot of our beds," she told me. "It's clear to me that the vision of the lady is not solid, and, in fact, we can see through her to the night-light by the entrance door to the cabin."

"Do you feel the lady means to harm you or the other girls?" I asked.

"No," she replied. Rather, the lady seemed to appear anytime Evelyn's blanket fell off, and would proceed, with her ghostly hands, to cover her.

The eeriest part of the story was Evelyn's description of the old lady's face:

"The lady has an almost motherly smile and yet, at the same time, has an evil grimace."

Chills crept down my spine.

After one such sighting, the youngest dancer, Bernila, couldn't handle it anymore, so she decided to leave the ship. Bernila never returned and never communicated with any of us ever again.

In my years on the *Pearl*, there were many deaths, both on and off the ship. After a while, those deaths began to have a profound emotional effect on me, pushing me closer to accepting the stories of the ghosts of the *Pearl*. It wasn't just the deaths themselves, but also other strange circumstances that may have catalyzed the supernatural occurrences happening around us.

Once, when on a shore excursion to Beijing, a passenger died— fortunately the ship's doctor was on hand to deal with the situation. Unlike the rest of the ship's friendly crew, Dr. Peter Distel, a German, was a very cold cookie. He stood six feet, five inches tall, had blond hair and blue eyes, and was fit as a bottom sheet. He relished his position on board the ship, and particularly enjoyed performing surgery and slicing into people. I recall one time I had to get a mole removed from my armpit. During the surgery, Peter said, "How weak you Americans are—your tear ducts flowing when you watch *The Sound of Music*."

However, in the situation that unfolded during this excursion to Beijing, Peter's dispassion was—you might say—just what the doctor ordered.

First, some context: to get to Beijing from the ship, we had to take a four-hour train ride from the port of Dalian, so it was not just a matter of walking back onto the ship. A decision had to be made whether to find a way to return the dead passenger to the ship or allow his body to be taken into the custody of the Chinese government. Since he was a

US citizen, it would have taken months, years, or perhaps all of eternity for his body to be returned to his family.

The passenger had passed away in his sleep, and before calling for the Chinese authorities, his wife decided to contact me, since I was leading the tour. In turn, I immediately contacted Dr. Distel, who fortunately was on the tour as well. The conversation was intense, as we were just an hour away from boarding the bus to head to the train station. I understood that it was probably a bad idea to turn his body over to the Chinese, but on the other hand, just how could we keep him "alive" on the four-hour train ride back to the ship and fool the Chinese in the process?

After a fast and furious exchange of ideas, we decided to bring him back to the ship and, ultimately, take his body to our home port of British Hong Kong. To achieve this, we had to pull off a *Weekend at Bernie's*-style maneuver, in which the ship's doctor and I pretended the passenger was still alive but extremely drunk.

At that time, China offered tourists just two choices for beverages— hot orange soda or beer, so it was not unusual for passengers to drink a bit too much. We got the passenger on the train, where he slouched between us for the entirety of the four-hour ride back to the ship. It was an extremely hot day in Beijing, and the train was not air conditioned. As you can imagine, the pungent smell of the passenger's corpse grew stronger by the minute.

When a Chinese official asked, "What is wrong with the passenger?"

we replied, "He had too much beer," and laughed. It was truly horrific. Getting him up the stairs to the ship and across the gangplank was the final challenge: we were literally carrying 280 pounds of dead weight. We did finally get him back on the ship, and he took his place in the meat freezer until we reached port in Hong Kong.

His physical body had disembarked, but did his spirit join the rest of our ghostly passenger list?

Another bizarre incident happened when I was hosting the ship's passenger talent show. I will never forget a passenger who was going on stage to sing. He was a very funny Jewish American gentleman named Jack, with an upbeat, happy-go-lucky attitude. Jack and his wife, Marcie, had traveled all the way from New Jersey. You could tell that even though he owned a law firm, he would have been happier had he been able to sing for a living.

The talent show, the finale to the entire trip, took place on the dance floor in the ship's main lounge on the final night of the cruise. It was a large space that held four hundred passengers in a semicircle. Jack told me he was particularly excited to be performing with our live band.

I always enjoyed getting to know the passengers and introducing their performances. Of course it was always a mixed bag talentwise, but nevertheless a fun event. As the lights dimmed and the orchestra played the overture, I could see Jack was excited, as he seemed to be going over his song in his mind.

Everything was going great. Jack was scheduled to be the third performer. Just before I walked on to introduce him, he asked me, "Can I tell a joke?"

"What joke do you want to tell?" I asked.

"I'm going to tell the audience that I wanted to sing the song 'Over There' but decided not to, because the band had already been there."

Our band was Welsh, and so he thought it would be a funny thing to say. I didn't see the humor in it, but of course it was okay. I walked on stage and introduced him.

As he walked into the spotlight, Jack literally dropped dead on the stage right in front of me.

The audience, in shock, went completely silent.

Then, whispers among themselves.

I requested that the stage lights be lowered and the band play quiet music. Finally, Peter Distel and his nurse arrived on the scene. Before they had even placed the Ambu bag over Jack's mouth, his tongue had swollen and his stomach was bloated. It was obvious to Peter, the nurse, and me that the passenger was gone. However, once again, the illusion of joy had to be maintained, so Peter and the nurse pretended Jack was still breathing as they transported him to his destination in the meat freezer, while I led the audience in prayer and then restarted the show.

The very next week, in rehearsal for the talent show, an older man slowly walked into the showroom. Albert was a retired college professor interested in Asian history; he had enjoyed his time exploring China a great deal. Now in his early eighties, he spoke almost in a whisper.

"Albert, what do you want to do in the show?" I asked him.

"I want to tell the very old joke about the snake with no pit to hiss in," he said.

I told him fine, and that I would see him at the evening show.

As he walked out, shuffling his aged feet across the dance floor toward the exit, he fell dead on the spot. For the second week in a row, a person had told me a joke and then died immediately thereafter. Once again, the passengers who were watching were in shock, and once again the ship's doctor showed up and pretended the deceased was still alive as he took him below deck to the meat freezer.

To this day, I jokingly caution people not to tell me a joke.

It took me years to get over the psychological impact of these events. Meanwhile, life on the *Pearl* continued to get darker. Perhaps the most dramatic of all deaths on the ship took place in Cabin 606, a deluxe suite that was the largest cabin on board, complete with a private balcony. Cabin 606 was called the Queen's Suite, and it had a separate bedroom and private dining area. Located midship, it was also the most stable spot to be during rough days at sea. Many times we would confront typhoons in the China Sea, and the ship would be battered by thirty-foot waves. Ropes were placed throughout the hallways so passengers could grab hold, and paper plates were used at meals to avoid breakage.

During one cruise, a very well-to-do couple in their early fifties,

Katherine and Grant, were staying in that cabin, celebrating their twenty-fifth wedding anniversary. Katherine and Grant were real estate moguls who lived in a mansion in Brentwood Park, California. To the crew, they seemed so in love—holding hands, smiling, engaged in deep discussions.

However, as the two-week cruise continued, things began to change, and it would later become clear that their relationship was, as they say, on the rocks. Passengers in the adjoining cabins were hearing Grant's low baritone voice yelling and Katherine countering in her high-pitched voice. Security was summoned on several occasions to request that they pipe down.

On the final night of the cruise, after they had consumed several bottles of Dom Pérignon, they had their final argument. Once again, nearby passengers were unsettled by Grant's shouting. From Katherine, they heard bloodcurdling screams, as if she were in excruciating pain.

Security, summoned once again, hurried to the scene, but too late: Grant had beaten his wife to death with an empty champagne bottle. The cabin was drenched in blood, and what was left of Katherine's bludgeoned face was no longer recognizable. But that wasn't the end of it: before security could breach the cabin door, Grant had taken his own life, jumping off the stateroom's balcony into the freezing waters of the Sea of Japan. The ship circled for hours in a search-and-rescue pattern before senior officers finally concluded that Grant was lost at sea forever. Katherine, meanwhile, was transported to the meat freezer. So much blood saturated the stateroom carpets and walls that no amount of scrubbing could hide what had occurred there. The cabin had to be closed off for almost a year, until the ship went into dry dock, where workers could strip and replace all the surfaces.

Interestingly, about a year later, movie star Elizabeth Taylor would stay in that same cabin, oblivious to the hideous violence that had transpired there. As has been reported so many times, Elizabeth lived a tumultuous private life, with many failed marriages, and had survived the deaths of many close friends. I have always wondered if Elizabeth was somehow subconsciously drawn to that cabin by its strange spirit energy.

Through the following months, supernatural encounters on board the ship continued unabated. As I correlated the stories of the various crew members, I began to realize that many of the spirit encounters were centered on the general area of Cabin 606 and on cabins and public lounges on decks directly below, above, or near that location. These stories included reports of the sighting of an older lady dressed in a white gown. I began to believe she might be the spectral image of Katherine.

In the crew bar, stories of sightings of ghosts and the legend of the "Lady in White" continued to grow. One night I was sitting with the hotel manager, Fabrizio Cavallone, a soft-spoken Italian who, although married, enjoyed the company of the female passengers. Fabrizio began telling me about how he was having difficulty keeping some of the Filipino crew in line. They were excellent workers, he said, but sightings of spirits in cabins, hallways, and other public spaces were starting to affect their emotions. Many female members of the crew in particular wanted to leave the ship. Understand, they all lived in the

Philippines, where the economy was troubled and profitable employment opportunities were hard to come by, so for a crew member to want leave was striking.

Fabrizio was not a believer in the spirit world, so simply could not understand what all the fuss was about. The *Pearl* would be docking in Manila in a few days, and Fabrizio was concerned that many members of the crew would simply walk off the job.

He told me about sightings by various crew members in many parts of the ship, but perhaps the most bizarre one happened in the engine room, where the skeleton crew had been working a long shift through the night. It was approaching 3:00 a.m., and the crew members were exhausted, pining for sleep. It was a particularly rough night at sea, and the aft of the ship was jumping in and out of the ocean, each time the massive propellers slicing through the air. The engine room was boiling hot and stank of fuel. It took a special kind of person to work within the claustrophobic confines of the aging engine room under even the best of circumstances.

On this particular night, the portside propeller shaft was malfunctioning, and the crew had been trying to isolate the reason. If they didn't succeed, they'd have to shut the engine down entirely—

always a dangerous thing to do in rough seas.

Felix, the assistant to the chief engineer, was in charge. He had considered contacting the chief, but decided to persevere and find his own solution. Felix had worked on many ships in Asia and was skilled at what he did, but no matter what he tried, it didn't work. Finally, out of the corner of his sweat-covered eye, he spotted someone or something sitting on one of the propeller shafts. Whatever it was, it was immobile, as if stuck to the shaft.

Felix's first impulse was to run off in the other direction, or at least ignore the dark figure, but he somehow marshaled up the courage to confront it. However, as he approached the entity, it vanished, as if it were only a figment of his imagination to begin with.

My suspicion, which I shared with Fabrizio, was that it was a "shadow person," also known as a shadow figure or black mass: a humanoid-shaped spirit or other supernatural entity seen only fleetingly, perhaps out of the corner of one's eye or peeking around a corner or doorway, before vanishing.

The strangest part of the story is that when Felix arrived at the spot he had expected the phantom figure to be, he discovered that it was the exact location of the origin of the engine trouble, which turned out to be bearings that were about to seize up. If the bearings had in fact seized, the propeller shaft would have been unable to function until we reached dry dock, and we could have found ourselves in deep trouble, adrift in the rough sea.

Was the shadow person a crew member from the past still tending to his beloved engine room? Or was it a malevolent spirit who had died a tragic death aboard the ship and had triggered the malfunction as revenge? We'll never know, but I will tell you that when Felix finished his tour of duty that season, he disembarked at Manila and never returned to the ship.

Another ghostly encounter took place in the public lounge down the hall from Cabin 606 over several days, always around 3:00 a.m.— the same time as the engine-room incident. Most people believe midnight is the "witching hour," probably because horror films and novels typically portray it as such. In reality, among those involved in ghost hunting, it is well-known that 3:00 a.m. is the real witching hour.

Lounges on a cruise ship are the center of emotional energy and group activities, and bartenders are the ambassadors of happiness. At that early-morning hour, they are busy cleaning up the bar and lounge, taking inventory, and preparing for the next day.

One afternoon, while the passengers were ashore, I was in the lounge drinking a soda, and Sulbert, the lead bartender, was on duty. He shared with me yet another story of strange occurrences aboard the ship:

The previous night, Sulbert was going about his usual duties when he suddenly heard strange music floating from the bandstand behind the dance floor. At first he ignored the sound, since it wasn't unusual for one of the musicians from the band to practice late at night. The sound was barely audible, but definitely identifiable as music. Sulbert looked up, and what he saw out on the dance floor astonished him: an ethereal apparition forming in the shape of a lady in a white gown. His eyes glued to the ghostly visage, he watched as the apparition began to perform a dance macabre. The Lady in White twirled in a ghostly waltz, like a whirling dervish from the netherworld. In shock, and concerned about his own sanity, Sulbert called for security, but by the time the team arrived, the Lady in White had vanished into the curtains, dissipating into a white mist. To protect Sulbert and his job, the security officers never reported the incident to the captain.

The final and most dramatic ghost encounter happened one night as we were traveling through the waters of Vietnam. It was always at night that we traveled through that area, for several reasons. For one, it was actually illegal at the time to do so, though it was common knowledge among the crew that the captain regularly took this route because it saved fuel and time as we headed from Indonesia to China. There was another, more serious reason to avoid these waters: heavily armed pirates, always on the lookout for modern-day treasures. Our ship, with its wealthy passengers and their lode of valuables, was a tempting target.

While cruising through the area, we always rotated our running lights to focus on the surrounding water, on the lookout for these marauders. On one particular cruise, near the end of my time on the

Pearl, we were once again skirting the waters of Vietnam and, as usual, staying just beyond the reach of the pirates. We had done this so many times through my years that it had become of little concern to crew members, so I, along with most of the passengers and off-duty crew, had long since gone to bed for the night.

Once again we were approaching the witching hour of 3:00 a.m. All of a sudden, we were jolted awake—not by the ship's alarm, but by the silence of the ship's engines, which had been shut down. When you live on a ship, the unending vibrations of the engines and the propellers churning through the water are constant reminders that everything is okay. When they stop, unless you're in port, crew members sense something is seriously wrong; even if we are asleep, an inner alarm goes off. I knew at once there was an emergency and that all hands would be needed on deck as quickly as possible.

As an entertainer, I lived in a passenger cabin on A Deck in the aft section of the ship. It was a small cabin, perhaps eight feet wide by sixteen feet deep, so I knew the layout like the back of my hand. When the engines stopped, I quickly threw on whatever clothes I could find in the darkness.

As I turned toward the door of the cabin, all of the stories of the Lady in White suddenly became a reality in my life. There she was, standing in front of me, a solid, full-body apparition.

Whatever serious emergency awaited me on deck was eclipsed by this otherworldly moment in time. Perhaps she herself was responding to the emergency in her own mysterious and terrifying way. As she stood there in front of me, blocking my exit, she appeared to be screaming, with her mouth opened wider than humanly possible. Her face was filled with stretched-out wrinkles; her body was positioned in what seemed to be a painfully strained, inhuman position. But the most unnerving part of the whole encounter was that although I could see she was screaming, no sound emerged from her mouth. It was a scream of intense, ghostly silence. I was frozen in place. I needed to get on deck, but I was blocked in the darkness by the Lady in White.

Then, in the blink of an eye, she was gone. My doorway was clear.

I hurried out the door and up the stairs. When I reached my emergency station on the promenade, I saw that a fire had erupted in one of the lifeboats hanging above the forward portside deck, raging out of control, ashes blowing across the wooden deck and threatening to spread the blaze and ultimately destroy the ship. Short of hitting an iceberg, fire on a ship poses the greatest threat at sea. It became imperative that the ship be stopped dead in the water, as that was the only way to blunt the winds created by the ship's movement.

As we came to a full stop, a strange silence surrounded the ship. On any other night, the clear, moonlit sky and calm sea would have been a beautiful, calming presence, but on this night it was the ship's worst enemy. It suddenly dawned on us that the blazing lifeboat was a beacon of light for the pirate ships rapidly approaching from the distance. We were in a race against time: the longer we stayed at full stop, the closer the pirates came.

The fire had to be fully extinguished before we could restart the engines and begin moving again, to keep the fire from flaring up all over again. The pirate ships were less than a football field away when the captain finally ordered the engines to engage, and the ship slowly accelerated to full speed ahead.

Emergency averted, thanks to the amazing efforts of the crew. The pirates would have to wait for another day to steal their treasure.

The next day, after a restless night of tortured sleep, I felt compelled to share my encounter with the Lady in White with other crew members. While breakfasting in the crew dining room, I was surprised to find out that several other crew members had had the same experience I had on that fateful night: they too had abruptly awoken in their cabins to the apparition of the phantom lady. While we were sharing our experiences, it suddenly dawned on me that perhaps the apparition was not trying to hurt or even scare any of us, but rather the exact opposite: perhaps she was a ghostly mother to the crew who stayed behind to dance the anniversary dance she was denied in life and, in the end, maybe even attempted to wake us up to save the ship from burning to the bottom of the ocean. Perhaps, after having met a violent, traumatic end, she was anchored to the ship, which had become her home in the afterlife.

Was it the actions of the Lady in White that saved the ship? After all, it was her home.

I will never know.

Not long after the events of that night, my contract on the *Pearl* ended, and I headed back to the States. A couple of months after my departure, the ship was sold off to another company, but it would never again be a successful cruise ship. Eventually the ship was put into mothballs, rusting and decaying in a ship graveyard, its glory days long over.

Through the years, I have often wondered if the Lady in White is still dancing her dance macabre on the now dark and hollow dance floor in the deteriorating hull of the once opulent ship. Was Jack still singing to an applauding audience of spirits, and was the shadow person still at work in the now silent engine room? If so, were they happy to finally have the *Pearl* all to themselves?

I will never forget my personal encounter with the screaming lady of Cabin 606, and how, much like the angel in the coal mine who had saved my grandfather's life generations before, she had saved my life and the lives of all the passengers and crew on that perilous night at sea.

—CHAPTER 4—

What Haunts in Vegas Curses in Vegas

I first visited Las Vegas as a child back in the 1960s, when it was a completely different city. Just over a handful of casinos and hotels dotted the strip, lighting up the dark desert sky in neon, with names like the Thunderbird, the Hacienda, the Dunes, the Desert Inn, the New Frontier, the Sands, and the Sahara, As a hypnotist, I understand that the first key to creating a trance is liberating the imagination. The casino owners of Las Vegas are looking to open up wallets and pocketbooks.

As a child, I was always expected to wear a suit and tie after six in the evening. Before I relate any more of my ghost stories, I'd like to share with you my first vivid memory of Las Vegas. I was staying with my brother Walter, who was ten years older than me, and my parents at the Thunderbird hotel and casino. My oldest brother, Laverne, twenty years my senior, was playing drums with his band, the Original Exciters, in the lounge of the hotel.

Unfortunately, since I was just five years old, I was barred from the lounge, accessible only to those twenty-one and older. However, I was allowed to watch performances in the main showroom, where food was served and the entertainment was family friendly.

On this particular visit, the starring attraction was the legendary Judy Garland—that's right: Dorothy Gale herself. During the day, Walter and I swam in the pool with Judy's children, Lorna and Joey Luft. Judy was staying in the cabana by the pool in the center of the hotel. One morning, after she and her family had finished breakfast, I snatched the red fabric napkin from her patio table as a souvenir. I still have it to this day. Later that day, Walter wrote Judy a fan letter requesting that she perform his favorite song, "The Man That Got Away," from the 1954 version of *A Star Is Born*, that night at her show. My brother took me along with him to the front door of Judy's cabana. Walter knocked, and as the door opened, we were greeted by Judy's maid.

"Could you please give this letter to Miss Garland?" Walter asked.

From the background came a familiar voice: "Who's there?"

The maid smiled again and stepped aside, revealing Judy sitting in the corner of the room, having her hair done. The maid walked over to Judy and handed her the note.

"Hello," Judy said, smiling at us.

She opened the note, read it, and said, "Thank you for the lovely note; I'll see you both at the show tonight."

We were ecstatic. Never in our wildest dreams had we expected to actually meet Judy. That night, my family and I sat in the front row behind the orchestra pit, and at one point during the show, Judy walked over to us, looked at my brother and me, and dedicated the next song to Walter: "The Man That Got Away."

This kind of magic happened only in Las Vegas.

I could tell you so many more stories that were just as amazing.

The ghost stories I am about to share were not part of a formal ghost hunt; in fact, they happened decades before I became a proper supernatural investigator. However, they may be the most startling of all my encounters with the spirit realm, because they include two rare sightings of full-body apparitions.

Through the years, I have had wonderful experiences at the Hilton, which, in the late sixties and early seventies, was the hotel in Vegas. Located a block off of the strip, it towered above all the other hotels there. Early on, it was prominently featured in the James Bond film *Diamonds Are Forever*. All the biggest stars played the Hilton showroom, from Barbra Streisand to Liberace to Elvis Presley; there were more stars at the Hilton than in the Vegas sky on a clear night. I was fortunate enough to see many of them perform through the years, in part because my father sold cars to hotel executives and to casinos for giveaways. I actually saw Elvis perform thirteen times in the Hilton showroom. In the lobby of the hotel, you would regularly bump into stars who had come to see other stars. Once I met one of my inspirations, Gene Kelly, who had just come out of Elvis's show and had a beautiful showgirl on each arm.

Before we return to the spirit realm, I did want to talk a little about Vegas and the mob. The main casinos Dad did business with were the Hilton, the Stardust, and the Aladdin. I got to meet most of the men who did business with him, and who were the real life inspiration for the characters depicted in the movie *Casino*, starring Robert De Niro. The Nevada Gaming Commission held hearings on Allen Glick's Argent Corporation, which owned several mob-connected Vegas casinos; my dad's closest friend, Doyle Davis, the slot manager at the Stardust, was banned for life from even walking into any Las Vegas casino as a result of that investigation. One of my dad's clients was Artie Newman, entertainment director at the Hilton. The mob would regularly handpick entertainment directors at the casinos—"not made men," but people who made sure the mob got its cut of the profits.

Artie was always kind to my dad and to our family. He knew I liked Elvis, so every Christmas he made sure I got a card and album from him. Artie was a middle-aged man who seemed always to be in good health. I remember one year, as we were getting ready to head to Vegas for some fun, we heard on the news that Artie had been found floating facedown in his pool. There was no homicide investigation, but the MO screamed "mob." These types of traumatic deaths probably accounted for much of the spirit energy that has built up in Vegas through the decades.

In 1989, many years past the golden era of the Hilton, the hotel needed some way to lure visitors away from the newer, more elaborate venues, so it teamed up with Paramount Studios to create *Star Trek: The Experience*. Each December, I would attend the International Association of Fairs & Exhibitions convention at the Hilton, after which I would stop in at the *Star Trek* exhibit to pick up souvenirs for my son Wesley, himself named after the character Wesley Crusher from *Star Trek: Next Generation*. In 2003, after leaving the strange new world of the *Trek* convention, I headed out the revolving doors of the hotel and into the cold, windy night. As I headed to my car, I stopped on a concrete pad between the driveways leading in and out of the hotel as cars passed in front of and behind me. While I was standing on the pad, a woman appeared out of nowhere, and suddenly was standing right beside me. I seemed to sense her presence even before I actually saw her. She was on my right side, looking at the Experience bag in my hand containing Wesley's souvenirs.

"I see you went to *Star Trek: The Experience*," she said to me. "It's really a great place, isn't it?"

"Yes," I replied, "it's always great to be immersed in the world of Trek."

"I was on the television series *Enterprise*," she said.

"My son Wesley and I really love the show and never miss an episode."

"It was a lot of fun to work on."

Just then, a car raced by, nearly jumping the curb. I felt compelled to turn my head away from the woman and follow the car with my eyes. Then I turned back to her, intending to ask which character she played. One problem: she was gone, having apparently vanished into thin air.

At the time, I thought nothing of it. As I mentioned, it was cold and windy, so I assumed she had simply retreated to the hotel.

I found my car and set off on the three-and-a-half-hour drive home to California. I kept thinking about what role she played on the show. I knew I recognized her, but couldn't identify which episode I had seen her in.

When I returned home, Wesley was waiting excitedly for me and his souvenirs. He told me he had just received the new *Star Trek* magazine in the mail that day. We made an exchange: I gave him the souvenirs; he gave me the magazine.

I sat down and started to look through it. When I got to the back page, I saw an obituary for an *Enterprise* cast member who had recently passed away. Wesley to this day remembers what happened next: all of a sudden, my face turned a ghostly white. There, staring back at me from the magazine, was a photo of the same woman I had just met in

Las Vegas a few hours earlier.

Her name was Kellie Waymire, and she had died a month earlier, on November 13, 2003, at the age of thirty-six from cardiac arrest caused by an undiagnosed cardiac arrhythmia.

I had been talking, it seemed, to a full-body apparition. She wasn't what we expect a spectral image to be, but rather a fully dimensional person, just like you or me. I had to imagine that for Kellie, the time she spent on *Enterprise* was among the most special in her life, and she had wanted to share that experience with someone, even from beyond the grave.

Star Trek: The Experience closed in September 2008, just prior to the Hilton being bought out and rebranded as the Westgate. The memory of that night will live with me forever.

A year later, in 2004, I once again attended the IAFE convention. By this time, it had moved to the newer and far more modern Paris Hotel on the strip. Greg Bennick, a friend and fellow entertainer, and I decided to stay at the opposite end of the strip, at the classic Sahara hotel. On the second day of the convention, we headed back to the Sahara to change clothes before sampling the Vegas nightlife. Once again, it was an extremely cold night by Vegas standards—not the kind of evening to linger outside.

The hotel had two elevators, one next to the other, servicing the garage. As Greg and I approached them, one of the doors was open. Inside stood two women with cocktails in their hands. I remember they looked unusually somber.

"Could you ladies please hold the door for us?" Greg asked.

The ladies made no response at all, but just continued staring, and made no effort to stop the elevator doors from closing. When we pushed the up button, the doors to the same elevator immediately opened; the two women had vanished, but the drinks they'd been holding, just seconds before, were sitting on the floor exactly where they had been standing.

Greg and I looked at each other, puzzled. With trepidation, we entered the elevator and pushed the button for our floor. We were so emotionally rattled by what we had just witnessed that neither of us said a word. Would Greg think I was crazy if I told him what I just saw?

Finally, I said, "Greg, did you just see what I saw?"

"Yes," he replied. "What was that?"

Before I could answer, we reached our floor, and the doors to the elevator opened again.

Then, something even stranger happened: as we walked to our car, we saw the same two women standing in the far corner of the garage, staring at us with the same somber expressions on their faces.

We were chilled to the bone.

"Greg, let's get out of here!" I said.

"Absolutely!"

We hurried to our car, jumped in, and quickly locked all the doors. I backed the car out and headed toward the exit. A glance in the rearview mirror revealed the women were fading into the background. Once we had exited the garage and reached the highway, Greg said to me, "That was insane!"

"I'm shaking all over," I told him. "I can't believe what we just saw."

As we continued down the road, we kept checking the back seat, nagged by a sense that we were being watched. Evidently, however, the spirits had moved on. We never saw them again.

Who knows who those two women were or why they had chosen to manifest themselves on that night? Perhaps they had been killed during a night out on the town and were seeking simply to consummate their adventure. I was not yet an experienced ghost hunter; if I had been, I wouldn't have left the garage, but rather would have approached the specters to investigate further.

I have visited Las Vegas many times since those two events, but have never again witnessed spirit activity. Someday I want to return to those locations, bringing my equipment and skills with me.

Star Trek: The Experience is only a memory now, at least to those of us in the material world, but perhaps it still exists for Kellie to enjoy somewhere in the spirit realm.

—CHAPTER 5—

The Ghost of Walt Disney

The 1960s was a magical time in pop culture: yellow submarines, a family lost in space, a nanny named Poppins who lived in a cloud and flew through the sky, a Batman reinvented through the lens of Pop Art as a "bright knight" who drove a Batmobile with a jet engine, and so much more. One of the highlights of every week for my family happened on Sunday nights when Walt Disney presented his *Wonderful World of Color TV* show on NBC. Color television, still relatively new, was magical in and of itself at the time. When the show began, Tinkerbell would fly around splashing vivid colors all over the TV screen. For very young boys like myself, the show was a virtual journey to exciting places I had barely even dreamed of visiting. The real star of the show was, of course, Walt Disney himself, the creator of Mickey Mouse and the Magic Kingdom of Disneyland.

My family lived in Southern California, so Disneyland was almost in our backyard. We enjoyed it from the very beginning. The park opened in 1955, a year and a half before I was born. But even before then, my brother had convinced my mom and dad to attend almost as soon as it opened. In those days, the freeway system had not yet been completed, so what is now a forty-minute drive from Covina to Anaheim took an hour and a half through surface streets, orange groves, and dairy country. I can remember how the drive always seemed so long, as both my brother and I were so excited to get to the park. We probably invented the saying "Are we there yet?" Of course, by the end of the night, we could barely make it back to the car on our own steam and quickly fell asleep during the drive home.

Every trip to Disneyland was special, but for me one visit in particular stands out as a once-in-a-lifetime event. It was around 1963, I was six years old, and although my parents were always very protective of me and my brother, they did give us a little freedom to roam at Disneyland. In those days, the park didn't yet attract the massive crowds that it does today, and the concerns that parents face today of children disappearing or being taken were far less prevalent, if they were on the minds of parents at all.

I remember it was afternoon, and we had just eaten an early dinner in the Carnation Plaza area. My mom loved to shop anywhere, but especially in the stores on Main Street. I asked her if my brother Walter and I could go look in the Emporium (one of my two favorite stores in the park, along with the Magic Shop). The Emporium had miniature dioramas of Disney's animated films in the front windows and lots of Disney-character toys for sale. Dad always gave me a five dollar bill when we went to Disneyland, and in that era five dollars bought a nice souvenir.

The Emporium was divided into three sections: a large front area with clothing and all things Disney, a smaller section focusing on toys and stuffed animals, and finally a smaller shop with pricier collectibles and glassware. Naturally, at that age I was more interested in the toys, so I headed to the second section of the store. Soon, immersed in this wonderland, I lost track of time. Walter loved Mickey Mouse; like so many younger siblings, I always chose the opposite of what my older brother liked, so Donald Duck was my favorite. After carefully perusing all the toys in my price range, I chose a Donald Duck hat with a beak that when squeezed uttered a duck sound—I still own it today. I headed to the cashier to proudly present my five dollar bill and become the owner of an official Donald Duck hat. As I was waiting to pay, a tall man in a gray suit and tie stood next to me.

He bent over and gently asked, in a voice with which I was quite familiar, "Are you having a nice day at the park?"

I looked up, and there he was: Walt Disney!

"Oh yes, Mr. Disney, I am having the best day ever," I replied.

Walt then asked, "What's your favorite ride?"

"Peter Pan," I answered.

He said "That's good to hear. Well, young man, enjoy your day!"

Walt then walked out of the store and disappeared into the multitudes of people on Main Street.

Strangely, I was excited by this chance encounter but not in shock, as it just seemed normal that Walt would be at Disneyland.

I purchased my hat and hurried to tell my family about meeting Mr. Disney. I had no idea how unusual this experience was, or that it would one day lead me to the spirit world.

Unknown to me at the time, Walt had an apartment above the Main Street Fire Station adjacent to the Emporium, and he was very hands-on in terms of keeping an eye on the park. I have since been told that it was not unusual during that era for him to walk around the park to make sure that his vision for Disneyland was being followed, but it was rare for him to visit with the children in attendance.

Flash forward to about 2015. I was a novice ghost hunter and was getting in tune with the spirit world. I was at Disneyland with my daughter, Ilia, and her boyfriend, Mark. After a wonderful day riding all the attractions, we decided to go to Main Street to watch the Main Street Electrical Parade. We reached Main Street a while before the start of the parade, so decided to look in the shops. It dawned on me that in all the years my daughter and I had visited the park together, I had never shown her where I had met Mr. Disney almost four decades earlier.

"Come with me," I told Ilia and Mark.

As we entered the Emporium, I told Ilia and Mark that the store had been set up differently in the sixties, with a long counter that stretched the length of the back side of the store. It had been replaced with multiple circular merchandise kiosks and a smaller table in the back center of the room, by the cash registers. Each kiosk had four or five levels filled with stuffed toys. I looked across the room and noticed a merchandise kiosk where the cashier had been all those years ago. Drawn subconsciously perhaps, I led Ilia and Mark there. When we reached the spot, I noticed that the top shelf of the kiosk was filled, strangely enough, with plush Donald Ducks.

I told Ilia and Mark the story about the Donald Duck hat and Mr. Disney.

"This is the exact spot where I met Walt," I told them, pointing to the floor.

At that very moment, one of the Donald Ducks, seemingly of its own volition, jumped off the top of the kiosk and landed exactly where I was pointing.

We stood there silently, in shock.

No one else was anywhere near the kiosk. Further, no one else had been anywhere near the kiosk from the time we had walked in. There were no bursts of air from the air conditioner.

It was truly an eerie moment. What possible logical explanation could there be?

After absorbing what had happened, I picked up the little Donald Duck and placed it back on the top shelf. I decided to find an employee and pose some questions. Just then, a Disney employee entered from the back room. The name on her badge said Nicole. As I excitedly approached her, she smiled and asked, "Is there something I can help you with?"

"Have you ever had anything unusual happen in this part of the store?" I asked.

"What do you mean?" she answered.

I shared the details of my story with her—about meeting Walt Disney there when I was young and about the strangely animated Donald Duck toy I had just witnessed.

She smiled and, seemingly not the least bit surprised, said, "That is not unusual here. Walt actually spent a lot of time here in the store. It was one of his favorite spots in the park.

"Through my years here, I've experienced many unexplained things, especially at night after the park closes and I'm cleaning up or restocking," she continued. "I've heard a male voice talking to me, and many times, when I put merchandise in a certain place, I return later and it's been moved. I was the only one in the shop!"

Finally, she told me, "I am not the only one who has had things happen to them. My coworkers have also had many other things happen."

"Have any of you ever felt threatened or scared?" I asked.

"No," she answered. "In fact, I feel like I am not alone and always safe, as if Walt is looking over us making sure we are okay."

I thanked Nicole for her time and the information, and we exited the store. As we found seating for the parade, I pondered the strange events that had just transpired, wondering if Walt's spirit remembered me as the little boy he had met all those decades ago. Perhaps he, as a spirit, still saw me as that little boy. Did he remember how I liked Donald Duck? That I bought the Donald Duck hat? Was Walt offering me the Donald Duck that had jumped off the kiosk as a ghostly present? On some deep, emotional level, I think that was exactly what happened that night.

Although I did take photos of the little Donald plush toy on the floor, I regret that I didn't purchase it, probably because we were all in such a state of shock and surprise.

To this day, Ilia and Mark remember that experience. For me, although it is a bit of a haunting memory, it is, like all things Disney, also warm and comforting in its way, as an experience that touched my heart on a deeply meaningful level.

For a brief moment in time, a bridge from the next world connected the present to my youth in the sixties through the spirit of Walt Disney and the magic he continues to create from the other side of the veil.

—CHAPTER 6—

The Cry of the Donkey Lady and Other

Haunts of Old San Antonio

Historic San Antonio, Texas—home to the Battle of the Alamo and a string of old missions spanning miles—and the surrounding areas are a giant hot spot for supernatural activity, as there have been so many traumatic deaths there over the years, creating spirits with unfinished business. The first night of this particular investigation, we went to the ruins of what was once the Hot Wells Hotel and Spa, a luxurious hangout for the rich and famous, just south of San Antonio. I had heard about the springs from the San Antonio-based Midnight Paranormal Society, which had collected fascinating evidence of supernatural activity during hunts, and I was eager to explore the site, now a preserved historic park open to the public. My wife, Susie, came along to provide video documentation. She is from Poteet, the "Strawberry Capital of Texas," located about thirty miles south of San Antonio.

As a ghost hunter, I always do my historical research before a hunt, and my goal is to discover a unique angle to whatever I am investigating. In 1892, health seekers in South Bexar (pronounced "Bear") County had sought out what was then the Southwestern Park, with spring waters that reputedly healed rheumatism and kidney, liver, and skin diseases. But there's much more to this story, because right across the river from the hot springs is the original location of the first movie studio in Texas, Star Film Ranch. Sarah Bernhardt was among the visitors, while performing in Texas at the opry house.

Nothing remains of the Hot Wells Hotel and Spa today, but back in the day celebrities would visit both for health reasons and also just to party and have a good time: Rudolph Valentino, Theodore Roosevelt, Cecil B. DeMille, Tom Mix, Will Rogers, and Charlie Chaplin all dropped in at one time or another.

With respect to my investigation, there was one more site of interest: through the woods, about four hundred yards away, was where the Southwestern Lunatic Asylum once stood. The asylums of that era were often referred to as "snake pits," filled with so much trauma and sadness. We couldn't investigate the land where the asylum once stood, since it was the site of a new, private mental health facility.

The sulfurous water that filled the pools at Hot Wells was discovered in 1892 on the property of the asylum. The 104 degree water reeked of sulfur, and many people believed it held special healing powers. So much spirit activity has been reported over the decades in the area, a function, I strongly suspected, of the fact that the water for the resort came from the asylum. At the time of my investigation, three pools remained, though of course they no longer held water: on one side was the "gent's pool," on the other side was the "lady's pool," and in the middle was the pool that everyone shared.

It was a windy, cool late afternoon when we arrived at the park. We were lucky to meet up with Martin, one of the security guards. I told him we were there to conduct a ghost investigation; he responded that several ghost-hunting groups had been there before. I asked if he had any ghost stories he wanted to share.

He had several.

"On many nights, both myself and the other guards have seen a little girl here," he said. "She rides a small red bike from the far end of the walkway to this light post. She continues to go back and forth, at the same time giving an unearthly giggle, until she gets your attention, and then she quickly goes behind the building and disappears."

"So you actually were a witness to that happening? "I questioned.

"Yes, I heard and physically seen it."

"Wow, that's crazy!" I said. "I wish we could see that tonight."

"When it happens, she usually shows up a little bit past 2:00 a.m., and I am not able to let you stay in the park after 10:00 p.m." he replied.

"Yes, I assumed the activity would happen around the witching hour, at 3:00 a.m., so it makes sense you see her, because you're on guard overnight," I said.

Martin then shared another experience:

"I have also seen a man in the window on the second floor of the men's bathhouse. He clearly was walking back and forth behind the window and finally looking out."

Knowing that the resort had twice burned down, I asked, "How was the resort destroyed?"

"A boiler blew up, and a fire destroyed the buildings," Martin said. "It blew the top off of the boiler room. Some of the roof pieces still exist in the woods."

"That's terrible," I said, but Martin wasn't done yet.

"There's more," he said. "There's an older woman who only appears on foggy nights. She's dressed in a beautiful black gown and seems to be singing."

Hmmm, I thought, could it be Sarah Bernhardt still entertaining a ghostly audience?

At that point I was thinking that between the water from the asylum and all the tragedy that must have accompanied two destructive fires—especially the trauma for both employees and guests the night the boiler blew the top off of the boiler room—there was likely to be enough spirit activity for us to tap into on tonight's investigation.

It was getting toward sunset when Martin took us to the edge of the woods and pointed out what remained of the employee cabins. He showed us what was left of a stand-up shower that was part of the original hotel. I thanked him for the tour and asked if we could explore the woods and grounds on our own. He assured us we could, so finally it was time to embark on our hunt.

I hadn't detected anything supernatural during our tour with Martin, and since our time was limited, I decided to focus on the woods and the remains of the employees' cabins. Dusk was now approaching, and as we walked through the dense greenery, I came upon the ruins of an old structure of rotting wood. There was no roof and only partial walls, and on the dirt floor in the center of what was once a room, I spotted a decrepit wood cabinet. As we ventured even deeper into the woods, I began to feel a heaviness that deepened with every step, and I sensed that we were closing in on our search for energy from the spirit realm.

Susie walked around the corner of one of the crumbling walls, and I asked, "Have you seen any activity?"

"I've been doing scans on my EMP meter, but so far I've only seen moderate readings," she replied.

I pulled out my own meter and started reaching out verbally.

"If anybody wants to communicate with us, just beep the red light on the meter," I said.

Nothing doing.

It was now almost pitch-black, so I told Susie, "Let's make one more try before we have to head back to the springs to see if we can find anything."

Burdened by the heaviness, I felt certain there was something or someone trying to reach out. Since our electronic devices seemed to be ineffective, I decided to go old school and use dowsing rods instead. Susie's grandfather had been a dowser in Texas, helping to find water and oil underground, but in more recent times, the rods have been found to be sensitive to spirit energy, much like a planchette on a Ouija board.

Soon, the rods were literally pulling me to one of the remaining standing corners of the cabin. Believing we had found a hot spot, I switched from the rods to the Sono X ghost box on my iPad, which began generating random words in quick succession.

"Do you want to talk with us?" I asked. "Do you have anything you want to say to us tonight?"

The Sono X continued to generate its random pattern of words, so I changed my question:

"What is your name?"

"Dylan," the box said.

"What is your last name, Dylan?"

No response.

I repeated the question several times; finally, Susie and I heard the unmistakable reply: "Grant."

For some inexplicable reason, I then felt compelled to ask, "Do you know my name?"

"Mike," Dylan quickly replied.

Susie and I stared at each other, the hair on the back of our necks jolting to attention. Contact.

"Did you used to visit the hot springs?" I asked.

Silence.

"Did you like it at the hot springs?"

"Not really so much."

Stunned by the angry tone of his reply, I turned to Susie and said, "Did you hear that?"

"Clear as a bell."

"All right," I said to the voice, "we found out you don't really like it here, so thank you, Dylan, for talking with us."

By this time, we had begun hearing strange noises surrounding us in the now totally dark woods, and we had no desire to further anger Dylan. What those noises were I had no idea then and have no idea now, but regardless, both Susie and I knew it was time to head back to the safety of the hot springs before the woods became even more dangerous.

As we emerged from the haunted woods, the artificial lights of the hot springs were a welcome sight. The experience had truly unnerved us. Dylan's recitation of my name was chilling, because it wasn't stored in the memory bank of the Sono X. So how did he know?

Both Susie and I will never forget Dylan Grant's hostile response.

The next afternoon, we continued our ghost hunt in south San Antonio, heading to two famously haunted bridges. We stopped first for a brief visit with the old aqueduct leading up to Mission Espada, reputedly an active area for spirit activity. We hoped to experience a strange phenomenon that occurs at an adjacent structure known as the Devil's Bridge, located on East Ashley Road. Through the years, locals have claimed that a lot of spirit activity has taken place under and around the bridge. One part of the legend tells of a priest whose Native Americans parishioners were tortured and killed during the Spanish

Inquisition. The priest, feeling responsible, hung himself from a tree near the bridge. Their troubled spirits are said to still roam the wooded area surrounding the bridge. The ghosts of these Native Americans have been spotted many times under the bridge, not only by locals, but also by a Catholic priest.

Another legend tells of a young girl who plays under the bridge. If you drop a rock off the bridge, you won't hear it hit the river below because she catches it. I found some rocks along the bridge and lined them up on the railing, preparing to test the legend. I tossed the first of three rocks over the railing; to my amazement, I didn't hear anything hit the water. I threw another stone; once again, no sound of any kind. The third time was no different.

I did feel a presence of some kind, though it's difficult to articulate exactly what it was. The odor of rotten eggs burned the insides of my nose; the smell of sulfur has long been associated with demonic activity.

Unfortunately, the day was passing quickly, and we had to move on to the infamous Donkey Lady Bridge. We drove along Jett Road south of San Antonio, passing by several antiquated cemeteries, including Saints Oakwood and the Loma China off of Zarzamora Street. I have seen many cemeteries in my life, but the Loma China was remarkable. Located on a strip of land surrounded by undeveloped fields, it was fronted by foreboding gates directly on the main road yet are almost invisible to anyone driving by. The crumbling gravestones appeared forlorn, as if descendants of the buried had long since abandoned them.

We did not conduct actual ghost hunts at either location, but I will share with you the legend of the Loma China Cemetery. Dating back to the early days of San Antonio history, it involves a love affair between a rich rancher's son named Carlos and a beautiful Chinese woman by the name of Lee Hong. They fell in love, but both families opposed the relationship, so they would meet clandestinely in the cemetery at night. One night, during a thunderstorm, Carlos was coming to meet his love when lightning struck both him and his horse dead. Supposedly, both Carlos and Lee Hong are buried at the cemetery.

Legend has it, however, that their love has never died. Locals have reported spotting a specter of Lee Hong six to seven feet tall. Chinese folklore speaks of the spirits of women who endured unrequited love or were somehow wronged during their lifetime. If you pull up to the gate of the cemetery around the early-morning witching hour and flash your headlights, the legend has it, you will see Lee Hong appear in spectral form. Someday I hope to return to conduct a deeper investigation,

Time was short, so we continued on to the Donkey Lady Bridge. As we did, I noticed strange fencing on the side of the road, and alongside it old glass bottles, mattress springs, and other odd items. The address was 2781 Jett Road, and behind the fencing was one of the strangest structures I have ever seen: the steel girders of an unfinished five-story building, placed in no apparent order, shot up in multiple directions. It was surrounded by dozens of pieces of rusted equipment and encircled by antique school buses, and atop the large steel poles perched a collection of buzzards, as if they were conducting a group meeting.

Later that day, I would discover that the structure overlooked the woods where the Donkey Lady's cabin would have been at one time. I still have no idea what the structure was, but I have never seen anything like it before or since in all my travels. I found myself wondering if it had one day served perhaps as home base for a cult of the Charles Mason or Jim Jones variety.

By this point, Susie was gnawed by a sense of dread and eager to move on. I fully understood; I couldn't shake the feeling that we were being watched.

It was now very near dusk, and we finally reached our destination, the Donkey Lady Bridge—perhaps the most famous place in the ghost folklore of old Texas. No one knows the real name of the Donkey Lady, but it is said that she lived decades ago on a ranch south of old San Antonio near where the bridge now stands, along with her husband and three children. The husband was a gambler and often journeyed into town to find a game. That night, Lady Luck didn't go his way; in fact, he lost everything, so wasn't even able to cover his markers. He hurriedly made his departure back to the ranch, and it wasn't long before gamblers showed up to collect their money at gunpoint. The husband had nothing to give them, so the gamblers killed him on the spot and set the ranch on fire.

The lady and her children were trapped inside the house; the children perished in the fire, but the lady somehow survived. Unfortunately, her hands were burned horribly, to the point where they resembled the hooves of an animal, and her face melted into a grotesque visage resembling the face of a donkey. Henceforth, she became known as the Donkey Lady.

Since that night, there have been hundreds of reports of a Donkey Lady terrifying people on this bridge, perhaps seeking revenge on those who had killed her family.

As we approached the location, several locals were fishing off of the bridge. I asked if any of them had stories or information they wanted to share about the Donkey Lady. Richard Rodriguez, one of the men, had some interesting tales to tell.

"I've lived here about fifteen, maybe twenty years now, and when I was younger I used to come out here and, you know, play around, just do the Donkey Lady thing," he told me. "So this was the main road from up there at Jett and down past where those barriers are, but I guess it would rain so much and flood back in the day that people would have to take Jett Road around the area."

"I've heard there were stories of murdered people out here?" I said.

"Yeah, um, back in the day they used to dump a lot of bodies out here," Richard replied.

"That makes sense," I said, "because of the woods and its distance from San Antonio."

"They found a dead person wrapped up in carpet over there," Richard said, pointing to a spot just under the bridge.

"There must be a lot of troubled spirits out there, besides just the Donkey Lady?"

"Yeah, I've been out here and actually roamed the woods and stuff at night. I've heard things, you don't know what it is, but I have heard things that are not natural, things crawling and moving."

Night was near, so I thanked Richard, and Susie and I began setting up our equipment for the investigation. We had no idea what to expect, but it turned out to be a night to remember.

After setting up and doing our day's research, Susie and I returned to our vehicle to rest and eat some dinner in preparation for a long, cold night of investigation. Once night had enveloped the area, we headed back, and as we approached the bridge, some teenagers came running past us, screaming.

"Did you hear that?" one shouted.

"What was that?" another one said. "Is it following us?"

When they reached their vehicle, they took off in a literal cloud of dust, as if their very lives depended on it.

As experienced ghost hunters, we were "shaken, not stirred," as James Bond would say. However, we were excited about what surprises the night might hold.

There was cloud cover that evening, so it was exceptionally dark out there on the bridge. I began the investigation by employing my Sono X ghost box, to see if I could make verbal contact.

"Do you mind us being on the bridge tonight?" I asked.

Random words emerged from the ghost box.

"Do you mind us being on the bridge here tonight with you?" I asked again. "Is there anyone on the bridge that would like to talk with us? I know there's been a lot of activity here through the years of people jumping off the bridge and dead bodies found here, so I'm not just reaching out to the Donkey Lady, but also to any other spirits here. So if there's anyone here, please let us know."

A low voice came over the ghost box, replying with a single word: "Man."

"We understand you are a man," I said. "What's your name?"

Silence.

"What's your name?" I repeated.

To me, the response sounded like "Will," but Susie believed it was "Bill," so I asked, "Is your name Will or Bill?"

"Bill," replied the disembodied voice.

"How many years ago did you come here?" I asked.

"Seventy-seven."

"What's my name?" I asked,

"Mezmer," he replied.

The answer literally sent chills racing down our spines. Never before had I heard my last name uttered on a ghost box. Even more interesting is that as "Bill" manifested my name, he actually combined a female voice and a male voice in the Sono X word bank. So "Bill" said "Mess" in a female voice and "myrrh" in a male voice.

After that exchange, we were buffeted by a gust of cold wind, and all communication halted. I decided to turn my attention to trying to make contact with the Donkey Lady herself.

I have to say I had felt a bit uncomfortable throughout the day referring to this tortured woman's soul as the Donkey Lady. After all, she had endured a hellish final hours of life, and the appellation struck me as callous. Nevertheless, since I didn't know her real name, addressing her that way seemed my only option. Both Susie and I brought out our EMF meters, but before turning them on I felt moved to say, "Please forgive us for using the name Donkey Lady, but we have no other name to use to reach out to you.

"If you're here, you can use your energy to make this device react," I continued. "You can show us you are here."

I want to make it clear that there was no electricity on or near the bridge, so the only explanation for any reaction by the meter would be the presence of some supernatural energy. At first, we got very little reaction. But as we moved from the center of the bridge to the far end, the wind mysteriously stirred again, and the meter started acting up.

For some reason, I felt that rather than relying on the Sono X again, I should take an old-school ghost-hunting approach, so I whipped out a standard flashlight. I purchase my flashlights from dollar stores, as they need to be the old-fashioned type, so I can unscrew the front, where the bulb is located, just to the point where it's almost touching the battery, then turn on the flashlight and wait for the light to turn on. The theory among supernatural investigators is that ghosts are surrounded by ectoplasm, which helps them manifest in our world, and that the ectoplasm has electrical properties that set off various devices.

Slowly, our meters continued to register supernatural activity.

"If you are here, Donkey Lady, would you please flash the flashlight?" I said. "You just have to make a little bit of an energy connection between the bulb and the battery inside. Again, we want to stress we're not in any way wanting to insult you by calling you Donkey Lady; we simply don't know your name. But if you're here, flash the flashlight for us."

The wind got all riled up, carrying with it an indistinguishable but distinctly eerie sound.

Once again I said, "If you are here with us on the bridge, please let us know."

No words, but I knew in my being that the lady of the bridge was there with us. The sound mutated into a harsh, animalistic cry, and the air turned frigid.

"If you are here tonight, lady of the bridge, please light the flashlight!" I shouted into the wind.

Just then, the flashlight, which I had left lying six feet from us, turned on—though nobody was standing anywhere near it.

"That's crazy!" I said. "It just went on by itself. That is insane!"

Then, addressing myself to the spirit again, I said, "Thank you for letting us know you exist."

What happened next came as no surprise, at least not to me: the light turned off, the wind dissipated, and it suddenly became much warmer on the bridge. I have always felt that a spirit must expel a tremendous amount of energy to communicate with the living

Hours had passed; it was very late at night—almost morning—so we chose to end the investigation at that point. We were convinced we had achieved our goal: to make contact with the lady on the bridge, and felt the evidence we compiled was outstanding. Our Sono X session earlier in the evening also had yielded persuasive evidence. Bill somehow had known my last name, and finally, the evidence seemed to say we had made contact with someone on the bridge, very likely the Donkey Lady.

Susie and I made a pact to return to this bridge one day. And as we drove off into the dawning of a new day, we said a prayer for the lady of the bridge, hoping that she would one day be released from her torment.

—CHAPTER 7—

Prisoners of the Spirit World

Old prisons are known by ghost hunters and even those who work inside them to be epicenters of extreme paranormal activity. Of course, that should come as no surprise, given the trauma, pain, and despair prisoners endure behind bars. Many prisoners are themselves violent criminals who have committed unspeakable acts, and carry this evil with them inside the prison gates. Many live out their days with profound regret over the choices they made in life. Could it be that many prisoners, after death, remain imprisoned, in the spirit realm?

The Old Montana Prison is widely considered one of the most spiritually active penitentiaries in the world. Located in Deer Lodge, it opened on July 2, 1871, and closed over a hundred years later, in the late 1970s. Today it is a museum, renamed the Old Montana Prison, open to the public during daytime hours for most of the year. I have been fortunate enough to investigate the prison twice, and both times I was presented with convincing evidence of spiritual activity.

In the summer of 2018, I was performing at the Tri-County Fair in Deer Lodge. My wife, Susie, and I decided to do the touristy thing and visit the prison, located just down the street from the fair. During the visit, I struck up a conversation with Samantha, the cashier in the gift shop, and told her I was a magician and hypnotist at the fair as well as a ghost hunter. I noticed that the prison was holding a special lockdown event the next night. I knew my performances at the fair would preclude me from joining until much later in the evening, but

I told Samantha I would nevertheless love the opportunity to join in.

"I'll ask my mom, Heather," she said. "She's the one in charge of the event."

The next morning, Heather called to say we were good to go. Even better, we would not have to be with the group, but rather we'd be given private access that evening.

Walking around the outside of the prison, especially late at night, is an unsettling experience; it feels as if you're being watched by the spirits of erstwhile inmates who have since passed on. The night before our ghost hunt, I had decided to take a selfie during our evening walk outside of Tower Seven of the prison. At the time, I was unaware that Tower Seven was well-known for its spirit activity. I was standing in front of the steel door, which had a glass window reinforced by steel wiring. The photo, taken by the light of the streetlamps, was at first glance unremarkable. However, when we returned to our room that night, I took a closer look. Both Susie and I were astonished to see there was a shadow face looking through the window at me.

The next night, when we arrived at the prison, Samantha was waiting at the gift shop entrance.

"My mom is out leading the lockdown ghost tour, but she said you are both welcome to go anywhere you want and have fun," she said. "Also, you're both welcome to come and have some food at the snack area when you're ready."

I thanked her, and we immediately headed for Tower Seven. We stepped inside, and upon close examination of the window, we saw there was no image of any kind on the glass. I then began attempting to communicate with the spirits in the room using my EMF meter, but almost instantly the device went totally dead. Odd, I thought: before starting the hunt, I had intentionally put fresh batteries in the meter— yet now it was drained of every ounce of power.

We decided to move on, sensing that the spirits of the prisoners were asking us to leave the tower.

Next stop: the registration room, where prisoners would be checked in and have their ID photos taken. I thought to myself how sad it must have been to stand in front of that camera. Most times in life, taking a photo is a happy occasion, but not here. As ghost hunters know, both mirrors and cameras can capture more than just the physical image; they can pierce the veil between our realm and that of the spirits. In many cultures, including some Native American tribes, photos are frowned upon, as it is believed that a camera not only captures your image, but also steals your soul.

In front of this now antique camera, emptied of film and in disrepair, Susie and I turned on our EMF meters, and almost immediately we began to pick up activity. I decided to use the EMF meters in a way I rarely used them—to conduct a question-and-answer session. As I stood behind the camera, I imagined taking photos of a ghostly prisoner. We instructed the spirits who might be present to beep once for "yes" and two for "no." Susie captured the event on video.

``Is there someone in front of the camera?" I asked.

No response.

I waited a few moments, then repeated the question.

This time, a single beep signaled from the meter.

"Did you catch that?" I asked Susie.

"Crystal clear," she replied.

Just to make sure, I asked again for the spirit to signal its presence. Again, the meter . beeped.

Excellent.

"Did you like having your photo taken?" I asked.

This time, there was no need to wait. The spirit replied instantly: two quick beeps, meaning no. We could feel the energy in the room radiating. Unlike in some of the shows you see on television, these types of sessions usually are very brief, so I thanked the spirit for communicating with us. The meter beeped one more time and then became silent.

Next, I decided to pose for a promotional photo in one of the cells in the main block. I wandered around, going in and out of several of the cells, looking for the right visual. Inside each of the cells was decaying furniture, including metal beds, rusted sinks, and toilets. I finally was drawn to one cell in particular, with an old hand mirror on the table, which I thought would make a good prop for the photo. I noticed it had a thick coat of dust on it, meaning it probably had been untouched by human hands for a long time. The dust would help with the photo shoot, cutting down on the reflection in the camera lens.

As I sat on the old mattress and held the mirror in my hand, I felt a little nauseous. Sometimes I feel this way when I am occupying the same space as an apparition. Susie took multiple photos, until we felt we had enough. I got up off the bed and placed the mirror back on the table. Then I noticed something that literally chilled me to the bone: two words appeared to have been written by a finger in the coat of dust on the face of the mirror:

"Help Me!"

At that point, however, some of the people from the lockdown tour group were passing by the cell, and I instantly felt the paranormal energy slipping away. I knew instinctively that the moment had passed.

At this point, Susie and I were a little hungry, so we decided to visit the snack shack. On the way, we passed by several more cells, all of which were unlighted. We saw in one of the cells what appeared to be a static form in the shape of a rat, with a life-size human head, surrounded by straw.

"Any idea what that thing is?" I asked Susie.

"It looks almost real," she said. "I'm not sure, but I don't like the energy it's giving off." We were curious to find out more about this strange sculpture, and so we both decided to continue to the snack shack and ask about what we had just seen. After getting our food, Samantha's assistant, Lynette, filled us in.

"That's a sculpture from an art installation that happened a while back at the prison," she said. "The artist decided to leave the sculpture at the prison, since he felt it belonged here."

"Whose face was on the creature?" I asked.

"That was Jerry Myles, who led a riot at the prison."

Myles, convicted of murdering a traveling salesman in northern Montana, was the leader of the infamous "Jerry's Riot" of April 1959, when National Guard troops stormed the prison to rescue twenty-three hostages. Myles had fatally shot Deputy Warden Ted Rothe when the riot began, and more than thirty hours later retreated to Tower One with rifles seized from a prison guard, eventually killing both himself and his teenage boyfriend, Lee Smart.

"I felt very odd looking at the sculpture," I said.

"That's not unusual," Lynette said. "Many people are affected in strange ways by the it. In fact, the straw surrounding it multiplies sometimes overnight for no reason."

I was eager to know more about Myles.

"Jerry despised inmates that ratted out other inmates, and so the artist who did the sculpture interpreted Jerry in that way," Samantha said. "In fact, one of the other inmates had ratted on Jerry, and because of it, he lost his position as head inmate boss."

I asked Samantha if we could investigate Tower One—the "Death Tower," as it was now known. She promised to check with her mother and let us know.

While waiting for an answer, we headed down into the bowels of the main building to "The Hole," or solitary confinement. Known also as the Black Box, the room comprised two cells, both in total darkness. Inmates were given a mattress, wool blanket, and honey bucket. With only our phones to light the way,. I started to explore the cells and also tried reaching out to spirits, both verbally and with my EMF meter. Eventually the meter latched onto some energy, leading me to a hot spot almost dead center in the room. When I placed the meter on the floor, the beeping became frantic, registering some of the highest readings I had ever seen.

In need of some fresh air, we headed to the prison yard, where we spotted Samantha and her mom, Heather Gregory. I shared with them our off-the-charts readings in solitary confinement.

"That doesn't surprise me," Heather said. "Sometimes, full-body apparitions have been spotted in that area, but not of an inmate. The reason it was in the middle of the room is because you were making connections with Henry Edward Evans Jr., who was a minister to the prison and remains very protective of the inmates."

Heather agreed to give us access to the Death Tower, and even led the way. After unbolting the heavy wood-and-metal door, she filled in some of the details of Jerry's Riot:

The uprising, lasting thirty-six hours, was the longest and bloodiest riot in the prison's history. A total of three people died, and several more were wounded. According to Heather, Myles fired the shot that killed Smart on the stairs just below the top floor. Then, on the top floor of the tower, he turned the gun on himself.

"Many people have had very strange things happen in this tower," she said.

She cautioned us to be careful going up, as there was no lighting in the tower and the stairs were decaying.

The tower looked like a set from the castle in the movie *Frankenstein*, or some German expressionist film. Rocks and rotten wood lay on the bottom floor, and the antiquated stairway wrapped around the walls as we ascended into darkness, brushing aside cobwebs. I could hear the creaking of the aged wood below my feet. For both Susie and me, the uneasiness increased with each step we took. It was a fairly cool night, but by the second floor I had started to perspire profusely. As we approached the top-floor landing of the stairway, our EMF meters started frantically lighting up and beeping.

When we finally reached the top floor, where Jerry had committed suicide, I became overwhelmed by emotion. The lead-painted, peeling walls seemed to close in around me, and I literally had to lean against one to keep my balance.

"Can you feel what is going on here?" I asked Susie.

She nodded.

"There's definitely something strange happening," she said.

After a few moments, I could no longer handle the wave of spirit energy and emotion I was being bombarded with. I told Susie it was time for us to go back down. Heading down the stairs, I was overcome by vertigo and had to grab hold of the flimsy handrail. When we finally reached the ground floor and exited out into the prison yard, Heather was waiting.

She wasn't surprised by what we had experienced up in the tower.

"It's an extremely active spot," she said. "After the National Guard and prison guards broke in and found the dead bodies of Jerry and Lee on the top floor, they kicked their bodies down the stairs. They didn't give them any dignity in death."

This concluded my first investigation at the prison, but I would return a year later, in May 2019, when I was invited to perform my *Haunted Magik Show*, which was to be followed by a late-night ghost hunt. As the sun was setting and the prison grounds were falling into darkness, I arrived to set up for my show. One of the first things I did was reach out to the spirits of the prisoners, thank them for allowing me to be their guest for the evening, and invite them to watch and enjoy my performance. I then went backstage, where it was pitch-black. I turned on my cell phone light, and the first thing I saw—staring me right in the face—was the face of the Devil, with a hideous grin. I turned around; behind me was a skeleton. I shuddered.

As it turned out, there was nothing supernatural about any of this.

"What do you think of our Halloween haunt decorations?" asked Heather Gregory, my host for the night, who seemed to have appeared out of thin air.

"Very cool," I said, trying not to appear shakened.

My *Haunted Magik* show went well, after which I broke down my equipment and loaded out as quickly as possible. By the time I joined the ghost hunt, it was already in progress, in what was once the main entrance to the prison building. Heather and Samantha had led many ghost hunts in the prison through the years, so they were well schooled in where the hot spots were and how to incite spirit activity.

At first I was a bit taken aback by the guests themselves. As Heather was attempting to make contact with the spirits of the prisoners, a couple of the guests in the back of the room were cracking jokes about the whole situation. I have found through the years that you do not need to have a group of true believers for a ghost hunt to be productive— just people who are serious about it. If you have people who disrespect the process, it creates a negative atmosphere, and communication with spirits becomes extremely difficult.

Sure enough, during the early part of the hunt, the jokes continued flowing from the two men in the back of the group, and nothing phenomenal transpired. I could tell by Heather's countenance that she was not at all happy. We then entered the main cell block, which had three levels of cells. With Heather's permission, I split from the group, determined to do some solitary hunting. I proceeded to the other side of the cell block, walking from cell to cell, attempting to communicate with prisoners from the past, but without any luck.

Finally, I decided to rejoin the group, just as Heather was readying to demonstrate how the master levers at the front of the block could simultaneously close all of the cell doors on each floor.

"Everyone stand clear of the cell doors," Heather commanded.

As she pulled down on the lever, the doors suddenly jammed, refusing to close. She attempted to reset the lever and pull it a second time, but once again the doors jammed. It was as if the spectral prisoners would not allow the doors to imprison them that night.

"This has never happened before," Heather said. "I guess we'll move on for now."

As I trailed the rest of the group on the way out, I heard a noise that seemed to be coming from the third floor.

I gazed upward and couldn't believe what I was seeing: hanging over the railing was a full-figured shadow person, staring down at me!

He had no recognizable features; in fact, he was completely black, yet still recognizable as a person.

Then, in the blink of an eye, he was gone.

By the time we reached the next stop on the tour—the women's prison—the two jokesters and their partners had decided they had had enough of the tour and left. Finally we had a group comprising solely serious participants, and I had high hopes for more dramatic supernatural phenomena occurring.

"The women's prison is one of the most active hot spots in the whole prison," Heather said. "The spirits of the female prisoners are fine with other women, but I ask that you men are respectful, since they don't like men in general."

She pointed to what she described as the most active of the cells and asked, "Who would like to sit in the cell?"

Of course I immediately volunteered. I entered the cell, which was so dark you literally could not see your nose in front of your face.

"Would you like the door closed?" Heather asked.

"Absolutely," I replied.

I sat on the bed and called out silently to whomever might be sharing the cell with me. When nothing happened, I tried reaching out aloud.

"I am not here to cause you harm, so if you are here, please let me know," I said.

I sat in silence, waiting for a reply. I must have repeated the process for at least fifteen minutes without a reply.

Then, finally, contact. Out of the dark silence came two chilling words, in a low-toned female voice:

"GET OUT!"

I didn't actually hear the words spoken aloud, but rather they seemed to penetrate my mind through some kind of ghostly version of mental telepathy. At the same time, I felt something pushing against my back, as if forcing me to get up off the bed. I immediately called out to Heather to open the cell door.

"What happened in there?" Heather asked me once I had rejoined the group.

"I was told to get out," I said.

"It's happened before. As I said, the female prisoners don't like men coming into their space."

I will never forget the sound of that female voice in the cell, reverberating through my entire body and mind.

There's a phenomenon many ghost hunters have experienced when taking photo evidence called spirit orbs: a small circle or some other shape of light not visible to the human eye when taking the photo appears in the image once it develops. I had experienced this myself before, but nothing like what happened that night:

There is an auditorium/theater on the prison grounds essentially in ruins. You can see the sky through the decaying roof, and in the middle of the hall are gallows surrounded by broken rock and wood, where an inmate was once hanged. By this time, however, the real gallows were gone, replaced by a facsimile.

It was almost three in the morning. "The witching hour" had arrived. A chilly wind blew through the openings in the walls and roof. I could see my breath coming out of my mouth as a mist. Only a few of the tour guests remained. Although the theater's balcony had deteriorated to rubble many years before, the stairs leading up to it were still in place. I wanted to take one more set of selfies before the hunt concluded. Because it was an overcast night, it was pitch-black inside the theater. I decided to take photos using the flash on my phone. As I stood in front of one of the stairways, I snapped three shots. At the time, I was blinded by using the flash, as the room went from total darkness to extremely bright light in a second. While in the theater I once again was feeling the dark heavy emotions that I had experienced earlier in the night.

After heading out of the theater and into the prison yard, I took a look at the photos. Two of the three were unremarkable, but the third stunned me: in the brightly lit photo, you can see me and the stairway clearly in focus, but just off of my left shoulder is a perfectly round opaque glowing spirit orb. Even more amazing is that the orb is actually in motion and blurred, while I and the stairway are static! It is the best capture of a spirit orb I, or many of my ghost hunting friends, have ever seen in a photo.

Spirit orbs have long been established by paranormal investigators as a physical manifestation of spirit energy. Not all floating objects are spirit orbs, as some can be debunked as flying insects or dust particles. In the case of the photo I had taken in the theater, none of these theories can explain the orb. In fact, it is so clear and the orb is so bright and so obviously in motion that it is clearly a supernatural occurrence. I have shown the photo to other paranormal experts, and after close examination, all concur with my findings.

Perhaps the spirits of the tortured inmates of Old Montana Prison are still trapped inside its decaying wall, not realizing they are free to leave and go to the other side, truly serving a beyond-life sentence.

—CHAPTER 8—
The Dead of Deadwood

People often ask me if I ever get tired of traveling, driving, flying, or staying in hotel rooms. In a typical year, I generally tour to about seven states in the US and, on occasion, several other countries. Because I work fairs, festivals, and amusement parks, I present multiple shows a day, equating to between three hundred and four hundred performances a year. It has been said that entertainers "get paid for the travel and do the show for free," and there's a lot of truth to that. Some years I stay in hotel rooms almost as many days as I am at home. For many entertainers, the road wears them down, and some end up with substance-abuse issues that destroy their careers. Life on the road is not for the timid—it takes devotion to a dream and endless patience. Having said all of that, I personally look forward to traveling. I sometimes even drive eight hundred miles overnight from one gig to another.

One of the reasons I enjoy traveling is that my parents, Clarence and Freda, took me on many trips when I was younger. In fact, I first flew when I was just one year old, and in the 1950s, flights were long and sometimes very bumpy in the old prop airplanes. My mom told me that on that first flight, my dad got airsick to the point that we had to deboard the plane at one of the connecting airports and eventually finish our flight on a postal airplane. My dad also really enjoyed driving, so we spent a lot of time on the road. I'm sure that's why I still love traveling down a long stretch of highway on new adventures.

Ghost hunting has been a great stress-management tool for me on the road and has helped me avoid the negative aspects to which many of my fellow entertainers have sadly fallen victim. In addition, my investigations have taken me to places I would have never gone and experiences I would never have had otherwise. On a typical performance night, when I get done with my shows, I can usually find a possibly haunted location to explore near my hotel. After shows, entertainers are, in a word, "wired," and so need to find a way to wind down. Ghost hunting and otherwise exploring the unknown are my release, and never get old.

Both North and South Dakota are wonderful, friendly states to visit. I regularly perform at the Central States Fair in Rapid City, South Dakota, and I have also performed at both the North and South Dakota State Fairs. The great bandleader Lawrence Welk was born in Strasburg, North Dakota; I've had the pleasure of sharing the stage with several of the Welk stars, including Bobby Burgess and Ralna English. Welk was a pioneer in the syndication of TV shows and in casting both Black and Hispanic performers. Of course, there are many amazing sites to see in the Dakotas, in particular in the Rapid City area: Mount Rushmore National Memorial; the Crazy Horse Memorial; Sturgis, the biker capital of the world; and, of particular interest to those who ghost hunt, Deadwood.

The town of Deadwood, as fans of HBO's critically acclaimed show of the same name know, was illegally settled in the 1870s on land that had been granted to the Lakota people in the 1868 Treaty of Fort Laramie. A gold rush catalyzed its growth, and like all gold rush towns, Deadwood was lawless, wild and woolly, in its early years, and since the city existed outside the jurisdiction of US law, justice was sometimes dispensed—unjustly, shall we say? Gunfights and other forms of murder were rampant, both in saloons and on the streets. Wild Bill Hickok died in a gunfight in Deadwood and is buried in the city's Mount Moriah Cemetery, as are other legendary figures of the Wild West, including Calamity Jane. Through the decades, Deadwood suffered through several major fires and experienced steep economic decline. Ultimately, legal gambling saved the city, and today it is a thriving, family-friendly tourist attraction.

The focus of my trip to Deadwood was to investigate the historic Fairmont Hotel & Oyster Bay Bar and the Mount Moriah Cemetery, both known to host extreme spirit activity. Because the Fairmont is no longer a working hotel, I was staying at the Bunkhouse Motel on the edge of town. After checking in, I went directly to the Fairmont to secure my ticket for the night's ghost tour. I then drove to the cemetery to check out its hours of operation. Unfortunately, it doesn't officially stay open at night; still, I intended to return after I ghost hunted at the Fairmont, so I took an exploratory walk through the grounds to map out my evening investigation. I wanted to know in particular where Wild Bill and Calamity Jane were buried, as those were to be the centerpieces of my hunt. It would be dark when I returned later in the evening, as there was no lighting, so knowing the layout was critical to my safety. I then headed back to the Bunkhouse to prepare my hunting equipment and conduct final research for the night's investigations.

As night fell, I headed to downtown Deadwood. As I strolled down Main Street, I felt as if I had stepped into a time machine. I could easily envision Wyatt Earp, who once visited the town, walking down the street, looking for a gunfight. It was a cool evening, but certain spots emitted a much cooler aura—a likely indication of spirit energy.

The Fairmont Hotel was built in the late 1800s and opened in 1898. Like many hotels in the Old West, it included both a brothel and saloon. The history of the hotel is very dark, especially the bordello. The working ladies did their business up on the second and third floors, but if they got pregnant and began to show, they were relegated to the basement. Some gave birth; others got abortions. Some died during childbirth; some died during the abortions. The basement, dark and filthy even in its time, breeded sadness and trauma.

In 1907, it is said, a sex worker named Margaret "Maggie" Broadwater took her own life by jumping out of a third-floor window. Why isn't entirely clear; I hoped to find out as part of my investigation. That same year, in a fit of jealousy, a man shot and killed a client of his girlfriend, another of the sex workers who plied their trade there. He managed to escape, but then accidentally shot himself and died while collapsing on the street.

Let's just say I wasn't surprised by all the negative energy flowing from the Fairmont Hotel.

The Fairmont still functions as a restaurant and casino. Often my hunting takes me to deserted or off-the-beaten-path locations or other venues that refuse access for paranormal investigators, sometimes requiring me to sneak in in the middle of the night, but the Fairmont actually welcomes ghost investigators. I have seen it featured on many of my favorite television shows, including *Ghost Adventures*, *The Dead Files*, and *Ghost Lab*. The hotel not only welcomes ghost hunters, but actually offers paranormal tours. If you're lucky, the current owner, Ron Russo, will be your tour guide; Ron enjoys meeting people and is a library of knowledge about the history of the hotel, its violent past, and its more recent hauntings.

Normally, I shy away from tourist-style ghost tours, since they rarely produce solid evidence; however, I was fortunate that Ron was kind enough to allow me to branch off and explore on my own. People have claimed to see the spirit of Margaret Broadwater, and my goal was to make contact with her to find out why she had jumped out the window and taken her own life. After turning on my EMF meter and temperature guns, I began to search through the rooms on the second floor, where the old brothel had operated. None of the lights were turned on, so the rooms were lit only by the streetlights beaming through the window shades.

I noticed that the wallpaper was peeling off, revealing many different layers and colors. Ron had explained to me that "the wallpaper layers were there from many decades and had never been replaced. As each lady took over a room, she decorated it with her own paper." It was like looking at the rings of a fallen redwood tree and seeing how many hundreds of years old it was, with each layer of wallpaper representing another of the women.

At first, I didn't find anything unusual. I was momentarily startled upon entering one of the rooms, thinking I had come across a full-bodied apparition lying on the bed, but then I realized it was merely a mannequin of a woman dressed in what would have been the garb of a working girl in the old days. I had to assume she was placed there to enhance the tour. I left the room and continued on to the next room.

Finally, my temperature gun jumped to life. Near one wall, the temperature dropped some twenty degrees—usually an indication that a spirit is present. Because the room was pitch-black, I switched on the night vision app on my phone. On the wall above a dresser, I spotted an old tintype photo of an elderly woman dressed in black; she wore her hair in a tight bun and had a severe look on her face. While snapping photos of the photo, I couldn't shake the feeling that she was actually present in the room and staring straight through me; it was extremely uncomfortable and unsettling, so much so that I felt compelled to leave the room.

Next, I entered the largest room on the floor. Taking a moment to calm myself, I sat in one of the chairs and began analyzing the photos I'd just taken.

Calming it was not: I could see very clearly in the ghostly green tint that the woman's face had been replaced by an image I can describe only as demonic, with dark, hollow eyes and an evil grimace. I had no desire to return to the room where her photo hung, but I knew I needed to take a flash photo of the picture to make a comparison. Hesitantly, I got up and went back into the room. Doing my best not to make eye contact with the woman, I snapped the photos and left, returning to the other room, where I compared the two images.

The demonic visage in the night vision photos was not present in the flash photos.

Perhaps dark entities cannot exist in the light, I thought to myself.

As I was contemplating the significance of this development, Ron and his tour group arrived.

"Did you find or see anything?" he asked.

I shared with him and the group the two sets of photos. Two of the women on the tour told Ron they did not want to go to the room with the photo.

"Do you know who that lady is?" I asked Ron.

"No," he replied, "The photos have been hanging here since the day I purchased the hotel."

As the group continued on its tour, I headed for the third floor. The front corner room was to be the focal point of my entire investigation; here was where Maggie had jumped from the window to her death on the street. I placed multiple devices around the room and down the hallway, including my Sono X ghost box, two EMF meters, and my digital voice recording device. The best spot to place myself, I thought, was at the actual window from where Maggie had leaped.

I sat quietly for a while, with the only sound being the random mutterings of the ghost box. Eventually I could feel a precipitous drop in temperature, so I started reaching out to Maggie.

"Maggie, are you here?" I chanted, over and over.

Finally, the meters started to light up. My ears detected movement in the hallway, the faint sound of footsteps, coming my way. I stood up and headed toward them. A gust of cold wind buffeted my body.

"It was him," my ghost box said.

"Is this Maggie?" I asked.

No reply.

I tried again.

"Why did you jump out the window?"

This time, I got a one-word answer:

"Pushed."

"Who pushed you?"

"Ned."

"Why?" I asked. "Why did he push you out the window?"

"Saw him kill," she replied, her voice even quieter than before.

And those were the last words Maggie ever spoke to me.

The ghost box went back to its random speech, and all activity in the room seemed to come to a sudden halt. Down the hallway, the flashlight switched on, as if the spirit of Maggie was departing. Then, just as quickly, it went dark.

I sat there for a while, too shaken to move. Finally, I packed up my equipment and headed down to the lobby, where I met up with Ron.

"Do you know if there were any witnesses to Maggie jumping out of the window?" I asked.

"One. Another one of the working girls in the brothel."

"After my investigation tonight and what I heard on the Sono X, I believe Maggie had witnessed a man named Ned kill someone, and then Ned pushed her out the window," I said. "Have you ever heard of a man by the name of Ned from that era who either lived in the hotel or in the town?"

"No, not that I know of," he replied.

"Perhaps the witness was too scared to tell authorities about Ned pushing Maggie, for fear of her own life being in peril?" I said.

"Of course," Ron said, "anything is possible."

My final stop of the night was the Mount Moriah Cemetery. As I drove up the mountain to the cemetery, I noticed that its American flag was still lit and flying, even at that late hour, which, for some reason, gave me a sense of comfort. As I turned off the engine, I thought of something the groundskeeper, Jerry, had told me earlier in the day:

"You might be interested to know that many of the bodies buried here were moved from the old Ingleside Cemetery, just down the hill. Eventually the land where the cemetery was located became more valuable as real estate, and so they moved most of the bodies up the mountain."

"What happened to the bodies that weren't moved?" I asked.

"Some graves were unknown or unmarked, and so just weren't moved."

"So you're telling me that there are remains of people under the houses down the mountain?"

"Yes," Jerry said, "they're still there. People continue to find human bones to this day in their garden or when they're remodeling their basement."

The thought of these bodies being taken from their "final" resting place and their graves being disturbed was unsettling. I know that when graves are disturbed, so are the spirits within them. I realized as I got out of my car and headed to the entrance of Mount Moriah that this was a place of not only sadness, but also confusion for the ghosts that lived here.

Mount Moriah is a large cemetery; in fact, it comprises many different sections. For example, there were separate sections for those who were Jewish and those who were Chinese. There was a children's section, and another for the anonymous dead.

I could have literally spent a month investigating all of them, but it was almost midnight, and I knew my time would be limited. I decided to focus on the gravesites of the two most famous residents of the cemetery—Bill Hickok and Calamity Jane.

I knew the cemetery had closed for the day, but I was hoping to find an unlocked gate somewhere. Sometimes on ghost hunts you have to cross the line a bit and take advantage of a situation. While it is always more comfortable to get permission to enter an opened gate, sometimes it just isn't possible. Popular ghost hunting television shows pay large fees or simply promise great exposure and good advertising to locations, so they rarely have to worry about access. It's never my intention to break the law, but I was able to rationalize my action with the knowledge that I was there not to disturb the residents but, hopefully, to give them voice and release them from the chains that bound them to this world.

On this night, I was in luck: the drive-in gate was unsecured, so I was able to walk in without any problem.

The grounds were lit only by the glow of the town sitting at the base of the mountain and the single spotlight illuminating the American flag. Clouds covered the sky, and it was markedly cooler up here on the mountain than in the town below. I sensed spirit energy almost immediately.

Wild Bill and Calamity Jane were buried next to each other, not far from the entrance. Because I was an uninvited guest, I had decided to pare down my equipment, which meant leaving my flashlight back in the car, having no desire to draw attention to what I was doing. For the same reason, I left behind the chatty Sono X. I did turn on my two EMF meters, but turned off the sound.

I placed one meter at each of the two graves and took a seat on the block wall nearby. In a whisper, I called out for any spirits that might want to make contact. The meters were quiet, and though the temperature was dropping, the change was slight rather than precipitous.

I believe that the trauma of a quick, unexpected death is a catalyst for a restless spirit, and Bill's death was absolutely that. Hickok had been an adventurer, wartime soldier, sheriff, marshal, gunfighter, and gambler by the time he arrived in Deadwood, where he signed on as a peace officer in July 1876. By then his eyesight was fading, and he was surviving more by his reputation as a gunfighter than by any actual proficiency at it. He was shot in the back during a card game; the cards he was holding in his hand at the time were black aces and eights, still referred to today by gamblers and magicians as the Dead Man's Hand. So to my way of thinking, Wild Bill's grave should have been extremely jittery, but after forty or so minutes with no action, I decided to pack up my equipment and just take a walk around the cemetery to see if I could pick up any spirit energy.

I held my pendulum by the tips of my fingers and decided to let it lead me wherever it wanted to go. Skeptics dismiss the use of pendulums, claiming that any movement that occurs is the result of subconscious direction from the person holding them. They call this phenomenon IMR, or ideomotor reflex. In hypnosis, we use pendulums combined with suggestion to great effect for many purposes. Here are my thoughts about using a pendulum for ghost hunting: I feel spirits may very well connect with our subconscious minds, and if so, why not use the pendulum as a tool to lead and connect us with the spirit world? For me, the pendulum is a solid old-school method that in many ways surpasses many modern devices in clarity of response.

As I held my pendulum, I felt pulled almost by a magnetic force. It was hard to see where I was, but I simply kept walking. At one point, the pendulum suddenly ceased swinging, stopping me in my tracks.

"Is there anyone who wants to communicate with me?" I asked.

I realized that I was standing in a potter's field, a burial ground for unidentified people or settlers who had come over from the old Ingleside Cemetery—no stones or markers, just the spirits of lost souls. And now, perhaps, those spirits were reaching out to me. In the darkness of night, there was no way I could have known where I was going. As I stood there, I heard a whining sound, as if someone was suffering.

"Are you in pain?" I asked.

The sound grew louder, but my question hung there in the air, unanswered.

"Can I help you?" I said.

As I stepped deeper into the potter's field, the sound seemed to mutate from whine to growl. To my left, I sensed movement. From behind a large tombstone shaped like a cross, someone —or something—was peering at me. All I could make out was the shape of a hood. It was like a photo out of focus, blurred and dark.

"What do you want from me?" I asked.

Bracing myself, I approached the shape, just as it dipped behind the tombstone. I ran toward it, but by the time I arrived, no one was there.

Did I imagine it? I wondered.

But my contemplation was interrupted by a deep, maniacal cackle erupting from somewhere in the darkness, growing louder and more threatening from one moment to the next.

I fled, stumbling and tripping over my feet in the dark. I was lost among the trees and tombstones, low branches smacking me in the face. I kept running, convinced that something was following me, even as the laughter faded into the night.

I don't know how, but I found my way out of the cemetery and back to my car. I don't remember ever driving as fast as I did that night as I escaped the cemetery—and whatever it was that seemed to take offense at my presence there.

To this day, that experience is the only time I have ever felt my life in danger from a supernatural entity.

Truly, Deadwood lived up to its name that night; the dead of Deadwood were stirring, with messages from beyond the grave. It is the fate of the paranormal investigator to sometimes be welcomed, and other times to be spurned—and to never be sure which to expect as you set out on your hunt.

—CHAPTER 9—

Ghosts of the Nevada Desert

Most of the time when I ghost hunt, I am fortunate to have my wife, Susie, or other paranormal investigators with me. However, there are times I'm on my own. The reason I prefer having a team is that the more experts are on the scene using their equipment, the more evidence you can gather. Additionally, having witnesses helps verify that events actually happened. When you are on your own, it's more of a challenge to capture those special moments that spirits seem to allow to happen for just a brief moment in time.

I was ending a tour in Idaho when I decided to pay a visit to a town I had always heard about from other paranormal investigators. Mining towns typically brim with ghost activity. Tonopah, Nevada, had a simple beginning: one night, prospector Jim Butler was camping out and had fallen asleep when his burro wandered off and found shelter near a rocky area. The next morning, Jim found the burro and, out of anger, picked up a rock to throw at the animal. Before throwing it, however, he noticed the rock felt unusually heavy, and upon investigation he discovered that the rock was filled with silver ore. Ultimately, that rock led to the discovery of the second-richest silver strike in Nevada history.

Unlike many of the mining towns of its era, Tonopah has not become a ghost town. Rather, it is a fully functioning town, with schools, restaurants, hotels, and other businesses. I booked myself a room at a beautifully preserved, Victorian-style hotel named the

Mizpah, rumored—of course—to be haunted. Not just any room, but a room on the floor where, it is said, Evelyn Mae Johnston—aka the Lady in Red—roams at night.

I arrived at Tonopah in the early afternoon, and I decided to scope out the town before checking into the hotel. It's always a good idea to get the lay of the land before nightfall and map out areas that may be of interest. I drove out to the edge of town to Old Tonopah Cemetery, which had been closed for many years. The cemetery is bizarrely situated next to the Clown Motel, about which you should know two things: one, each room is themed after a different clown, and two, it has been called the Scariest Motel in America.

I knew I would need to stop in the lobby of the motel to ask permission to conduct my investigation at the cemetery, and also to confirm how late I could be on the property.

As I walked into the lobby, I strangely found it difficult to breathe, as if my lungs were being constricted by some invisible force. The lobby is literally a museum of clowns, and I couldn't help feeling like I had taken a detour into *The Twilight Zone*. Scores of clowns in all shapes and sizes filled every space in the room, and I fervently hoped Pennywise wasn't among them. In the center of the lobby was a life-size clown dummy, sitting in a chair with an insane, Joker-like grimace on his face. If I had been able to spend more time in Tonopah, I would have loved to investigate the Clown Motel, but as it was I had just enough time for the cemetery, and truth be told, I wasn't unhappy to get out of there once I had the information I needed, so at least I could breathe freely again.

Inside the cemetery gates, I was struck by how small the graveyard was. I'd say only a few hundred people were buried there. Based on the tombstone dates, I deduced that many of them were among Tonopah's first residents. From the research I had done, I knew that many of the townsfolk had fallen victim to the Tonopah Plague of 1905. The cause of the plague remains a mystery to this day. Other cemetery "residents" include the remains of fourteen miners killed in the Belmont Mine Fire of 1911.

Sadly, many children too were buried there, and as I walked through the area where their tombstones were, I noticed that sun-weathered stuffed animals, covered in dust, had been placed atop each of the graves, in all likelihood long ago. The tombstones and tablets bore names like Baby O'Donnell, Little Anakeesta, and Baby Brooklyn, each of whom had died in infancy.

It was a strange, gothic visage, and sadness—common of course to any cemetery—seemed particularly potent here.

After mapping out my nighttime investigation of the Old Tonopah Cemetery, I drove back to the Mizpah. The hotel was built in 1905 and is listed in the US National Register of Historic Places, and the elevator, though modernized, had retained some of its older features, so that it evoked the days of the Wild West. When I went to push the button for my floor, I got my first surprise of the night: the button for the fifth floor was already lit up. I knew the elevator wasn't coming from another floor, because it was surrounded by a mesh-framed shaft, so I could see that it had been sitting there inactive, waiting to be summoned. Nobody had entered the elevator before me. It was as if the spirits of the hotel were letting me know they were present and welcoming me to their home.

Early that night I decided to get some dinner in the hotel restaurant before starting out on my adventure into the unknown. While eating I struck up a conversation with my server, Shambria.

"Do you know about any ghost activity in the hotel?" I asked.

"Oh yes, there've been lots of ghost sightings," she answered. "I've even had many things happen to me here."

"Would you be willing to meet me after work and take me on a tour of the hotel?" I asked. "I'd be happy to pay you for your time."

Fortunately, Shambria agreed, so we planned to rendezvous at 9:15 on the fifth floor. That left me some time to explore on my own, and since I was staying on the most active floor, I thought I would sit in the hallway and set up my equipment. I didn't have private access, but the employee at the hotel desk had told me at check-in that I was welcome to investigate any of the public areas in the hotel, including the hallways, as long as I was quiet and respectful of the other guests. In the hallway just outside my room, there was a lovely antique couch and chairs with a tintype photo of the Lady in Red, so I decided this would be my base of operations. Across the hall next to my room was where Evelyn Mae Johnston was killed. In fact, the exact spot on the carpet where her life had ended was just a few feet away from me. As the legend goes, the Lady in Red was a prostitute who was beaten to death by either a jealous boyfriend or her husband, who did not know she was working as a lady of the evening.

Many hotel guests through the years have claimed to experience strange happenings in and around the room where she had spent her last night. I turned off the lights in the sitting area and walked up and down the hallway. Unfortunately, I couldn't use an EMF meter to look for hot spots because of all the electrical wiring and light fixtures, so instead I used my laser temperature gauge, but came up empty. Pressed for time before meeting Shambria, I decided to focus in on the murder area of the Lady in Red.

It was all quiet on the hallway front for a while, before finally my EMF meter started to show some life. I thought I detected sounds emanating from inside the Lady in Red's old room, but couldn't make out exactly what the noise was. I crept up as close to the door as possible; somebody was talking. Make that two people—a man and a woman, it sounded like—conversing intensely, as if in an argument.

I knew the room was occupied that night by a couple of honeymooners, whom I had spotted leaving descending in the elevator just minutes before.

Eerie.

As I turned to head back to the couch, a strange phenomenon occurred; the photo of Evelyn hanging on the wall was warping—almost as if it was liquefying right in front of my eyes.

Also eerie.

Overcome by vertigo, I staggered back toward the picture and fell onto the couch. Was the Lady in Red reaching out?

Unfortunately, the meters went silent, and the dizziness dissipated. Evelyn and I would have to postpone our rendezvous until another day.

Not so me and Shambria, who arrived soon after and led me to the basement, reputedly one of the most fertile spots in the building for ghost hunters. As we traipsed down the stairs, my meters started perking up. Actually, "perking up" is an understatement. They went crazy, hitting 3.00, which is almost off-the-charts crazy.

"Nobody likes to be down here," Shambria informed me.

Nobody living, that is.

Shambria shared with me a story that had happened to her in this very location.

"I was giving a tour, and suddenly I got very cold," she said. "At first I just shook it off and didn't think anything of it. I had separated from the group and was standing where we're standing right now; all of a sudden, a very large man appeared, standing right beside me."

"Did he say anything?" I wanted to know.

Yes, she told me, one word: "Hey!"

Strange, I told Shambria; the same thing happened to me once when I was investigating a mine.

At this point my meter was rocking, all the way up to 3.88, one the highest readings I had ever seen.

Shambria next guided us along to a spot under the sidewalk in front of the hotel, surrounded by cobblestone walls. It was damp and chilly underground; the space was tight enough to make me feel like the walls were closing in.

"Do you hear that?" she asked me.

I did. It sounded like furniture being dragged across the dirt floor in the room behind us. Twice, we heard it.

I had placed my EMF meter in my back pants pocket so that I could use my phone to shoot photos and video. For some reason the meter started beeping, so I pulled it from my pocket and was startled to find that it had completely turned off—apparently of its own volition. Which might not have been a big deal except that it had just been registering spirit activity. This was a first for me, in all my years of ghost hunting.

"Creepy," I said.

But not as creepy as Shambria's next tale of supernatural adventure:

"I was giving a tour to a couple, and they set up a camera in this spot. The camera had a fresh battery. Then we went up to investigate the fifth floor, and when we came back, the battery was totally drained of all power. We were only gone for a brief time, and yet the fully charged battery was dead."

Again, I could relate: I had experienced a similar phenomenon at the Old Montana Prison in Deer Lodge.

But get this, she said: "It wasn't just that battery. They had four other freshly charged batteries, and each one went dead as they changed them out in their camera."

Onward we went, to another area of the basement, where there is an entrance to an old mining tunnel, prompting another of Shambria's stories:

"So I was leading another tour with a couple, and when we walked into the chamber the spirit of a tall man was walking from that ladder over there through this doorway and down this hall to the other doorway."

"What did he look like?" I asked.

Hard to tell, she replied. "He was in dark shadows, but seemed to be dressed like a miner."

Here I should mention that this particular area of the hotel was used to create haunting experiences every Halloween, and some of the props still decorated the room. At the doorway where Shambria had once spotted a ghost miner was a full-size wooden coffin, illuminated by light sneaking through the side doorway. As Shambria finished telling me about the phantom ghost miner, a curious thing happened: down the dark hallway, in front of the coffin, appeared a full-bodied shadow person. My imagination, perhaps? Except that we both saw it. He was present for a fraction of a moment, then exited through the side door, with me in pursuit.

Alas, as quickly as he appeared, he was gone.

Could Shambria's recounting of the tale have conjured up the miner? I would have to file that question under "unsolved mysteries."

Shambria and I soon parted ways. Outside, the temperature had dropped; it was cold and windy—a perfect night for ghost hunting in a cemetery. As I drove toward the parking lot of the Clown Motel, I noticed that the office was closed and dark, though as I approached on foot, I could see a collection of clowns peering out at me.

It was about midnight. I headed down the hill and through the archway of the Old Tonopah Cemetery, then spent about forty-five minutes checking out some of the oldest tombstones, to no avail. Some invisible force seemed to be pulling me toward the children's area, so off I headed. My meter seemed to approve, emitting some pretty strong readings. I kept moving toward the area where I had seen the stuffed animals earlier in the day, eager to discover whether any of the children buried there wished to communicate with me.

"Do any of you want to say something?" I asked.

No immediate response, but a strong gust of wind stopped me in my tracks. I looked down and saw I was standing in front of a grave upon which rested two strange little dolls. As I bent down to read the tombstone, my eyes blurred, to the point where none of the letters appeared clearly enough to read.

Over the roar of the wind, I could hear faintly what sounded like a child laughing, chilling me to the bone. I switched on my Sono X ghost box.

"What do you want to tell me?" I asked once, then twice.

The ghost box was sputtering nonsense.

"Do you want me here?" I asked.

Apparently not.

"Leave now," the box said.

I knew I had to get out of there. As the wind blew and rain started to come down, I left the cemetery as quickly as possible.

I had brought a flashlight with me but, despite the darkness, had refrained from turning it on, to keep my presence furtive. It had begun to rain, and as I approached the exit, I stopped to say goodbye to all of the children buried there and to wish them well.

All of a sudden, the flashlight switched on. I hadn't pressed the button, and that's the honest truth. But even stranger was this: had it not turned on at that very moment, I would certainly have fallen into a ditch that, I soon discovered, was directly in front of me.

With the help of the ghosts from the past, I safely reached my car and headed back to the hotel.

My trip to Nevada had proved incredibly productive. I had, I believed, overheard a conversation involving the famous Lady in Red, whose photo then warped before my eyes. My EMF meter had beeped audibly, despite being turned off. Furniture had seemed to move of its own volition in the basement of the hotel, where I'd also spotted a shadow person. Finally, my flashlight had exhibited a mind of its own by inexplicably turning on all by itself, thereby in all probability saving me from a broken leg.

My visit to the Mizpah and the Old Tonopah Cemetery will haunt my memories forever.

—CHAPTER 10—

The Tell-Tale Heart of the Clark Chateau

G host hunting, once relegated to B movies and fringe late-night radio shows, has gone mainstream. There are literally hundreds of television shows, YouTube programs, podcasts, and websites dedicated to the subject. In recent years, scripted television dramas such as *Ghost Whisperer* and *Medium* have helped popularize the subject of necromancy, or talking with the dead.

When people learn I'm a ghost hunter, the first thing they often want to know is what I think of some of the more popular ghost-hunting reality television shows. My reply is that they are designed for entertainment purposes. To start with, they focus on the ghost hunters as the stars of the programs, instead of the spirits, who should be the real center of the stories. The melodramatic acting and scripting often does a disservice to the real mystery and wonder of the supernatural. The "demonic" activity and violence that the hunters experience is way over the top and couldn't be further from what we experience in actual paranormal investigations.

Do I watch those shows? Absolutely; they are very entertaining, and sometimes I think they actually do stumble upon some valid spirit activity. But understand: it is unreal to expect to produce a one-hour show on a weekly basis in which ghost hunters routinely find ghosts and experience type A phenomena on demand. Spirits are not actors and do not respond like trained animals on command, and actual paranormal investigation is a painstaking process. So many investigations dead-end without activity or evidence, even if you are at the "most haunted location in the world."

As a ghost hunter, I have always approached my work as a detective, investigating as dispassionately as possible. I execute my work with forensic methodology. I use logic and the tools of the trade and collect evidence on voice recordings and video. I never take anything personally. The spirits and their stories are the center of my investigations, not me, and I never look for paranormal activity to have any connection with me or my family.

The investigation I will now tell you about took both me and, especially, my wife, Susie, completely by surprise. We literally had no idea just how personal the evidence and spirit activity we encountered that fateful night was until the following day.

In August 2019, Susie and I, on a break from touring, were staying in the Butte, Montana, area in search of a location to do some ghost hunting. Once referred to as the Richest Hill on Earth, Butte had once-upon-a-time made hundreds of people wealthy and provided scores of jobs to immigrants thanks to its abundance of mineral wealth. As a sidenote, I should also mention that it is also the birthplace of a particular inspiration of mine, the world famous daredevil Evel Knievel.

One day, while conducting research, I happened upon the Bozeman Paranormal Facebook page, and began following it. Bozeman Paranormal was created by Elies Adams, and as its title implies, is based out of Bozeman, Montana. In looking for something to do during our break, I decided to take a look at the group's page. Susie and I were in luck: it turned out they were hosting an event that week at the Clark Chateau in Butte. Participation was limited, so I contacted Elies, who readily agreed to reserve spots for us.

This would be a different experience for me, as I had never investigated with a group before. I was excited about meeting like-minded people, yet also a bit hesitant to be joining a collection of people I didn't know. Earlier that day, Susie and I had decided to do some sightseeing, focusing on locations with special meaning for her; she had visited the area decades earlier with her first husband, who had since passed away, and wanted to return to some of those sites.

The Clark Chateau was constructed from 1898-1899. I mentioned that Butte is known for its extensive copper mining, and the chateau was built for Charles Clark, oldest son of "Copper King" W. A. Clark, and his wife, Katherine. William Clark had spared no expense in choosing quality materials and the artisan decor of this French chateau-style mansion. Driving up to the chateau immediately stimulated my imagination; it resembled a foreboding castle out of some black-and-white movie from the vault of Universal Classic Monsters, the film franchise responsible for such thirties and forties films as *Frankenstein*, *Dracula*, and *The Wolfman*. As the door opened, I half-expected to be greeted by Bela Lugosi uttering his famous "Good eeee-vening."

Instead, it was Elies Adams who greeted me, with a warm, positive attitude, and dressed like Indiana Jones. Stepping into the antiques-filled chateau was like passing through a time machine, instantly transporting us into the past. Once all of the participants had arrived, Elies assembled us for a meeting in the entrance hall, beneath a crystal chandelier.

"Tonight, you will probably have a unique experience," Elies told us. "This place is filled with spirit energy."

She then displayed various pieces of ghost hunting equipment and explained their uses, finally telling us, "We will all work together as a team and help each other to get the most out of the investigation. I will be happy to help you in any way I can."

Essentially, we would work as paranormal archeologists, moving from room to room with Elies as our guide. She was intimately familiar with the chateau's history and could identify possible hot spots throughout.

Our first stop was the parlor, where a piano served as the centerpiece, surrounded by French-style furniture and artwork hanging on the walls. We set about employing our equipment, and as usual, Susie began to document the investigation on video. Elies's ghost box started scanning various radio frequencies in rapid succession. I circled the room attempting to pick up on a hot spot; with each successive circle, I felt drawn to the piano. Using my EMF meter, I focused on the keys. After a few moments of calling out to spirits, I noticed that my meter was acting up—signaling not in its normal, repetitive way, but rather emitting beeps that seemed to be playing out a musical tune of some sort as I scanned from one end of the keyboard to the other.

Meanwhile, Elies was interrogating her ghost box over and over with the question "Who is in the room?"

In response, the ghost box simply—and not very helpfully—churned out a grating white noise, while the piano's ghostly sonata continued to play.

"Do you hear this?" I asked Susie. "Does it sound like a song?"

"It does," she replied.

Elies heard it too.

"I've never heard an EMF meter respond in that way before," she said.

No matter how many times I hear a voice emerge from a ghost box, I'm still unsettled by it. And the disembodied voice that greeted us from another world was no exception:

"Robert," it said, at last responding to Elies's query.

Chilling? Yes.

A sign that someone was eager to converse with us?

I thought so, but whoever it was who had been tinkering on the piano decided at more or less that very moment to stop, and Elies's ghost box was suddenly pumping out meaningless status again.

Unbowed, Elies moved us all into the séance room, which looked just as you might imagine, with an oblong table in the middle, covered with a cream-colored antique lace tablecloth. The only thing missing was a crystal ball. I branched off into an anteroom, where I took a seat and attempted to make contact with the entity we had just encountered in the parlor. As I called out to him, the battery in my back pocket suddenly—and inexplicably—began heating up. In fact, it got so hot that I had to yank it from my pocket, and throw it to the floor. When it was cool enough to touch, I picked it up and rejoined my wife in the séance room.

Elies's ghost box, perched atop the table, was sputtering out unearthly sounds as Elies continued to inquire about the identity of the spirit who had spoken to us in the parlor. At first, no response. Then, contact.

"Bob," the spirit said this time.

This seemed to trigger a contagion among our EMF meters, starting with those at the end of the table where Susie was sitting. The sounds from the meters were quite noisy, so Susie decided to place her meter on her lap. At first her meter stopped beeping, but suddenly started up again while on her lap. This was unheard of. I listened carefully, trying to distinguish one meter's sound from another; I thought I detected a rhythmic pattern among them.

"Does that sound like the beeping of a heart monitor?" I asked Susie and Elies.

Both concurred.

Susie then returned her meter to the table. It too started beeping like a heart monitor, in tandem with Elies's, which was making the same sound. I readjusted the meters slightly so that they were facing each other, and they started beeping to an identical beat. If I moved either of them away from Susie, the beat would stop, but when I moved them back it started up again. This went on for some time, then suddenly came to a halt.

Remember all this, because it is about to figure prominently in our story.

We moved on to the upper ballroom, a large space with windows. Elies spoke to the group:

"Now we're going to turn off the lights, and I am asking everyone to remain silent for a while."

In darkness, we worked the room with our devices, searching for hot spots. The temperature dropped; nothing unusual about that. I noticed that one of the investigators was working old school, with divining, or dowsing, rods; she was a "sensitive," able to *feel* spirit presences around her. At one point, her rods started leading her in the direction of her friend Sue, but then turned away from her friend and led toward Susie.

"What's your name?" the investigator asked my wife.

"Susie."

The investigator then realized that it was Susie, not Sue, whom the spirit wanted to contact.

Unfortunately, at this time, Elies mentioned our allotted time at the chateau was nearing an end, and she directed us all up to a stairway where we had our final experience of note that night.

At the top of a stairway, we were told that a little girl had tumbled down these stairs many years earlier and died. Susie took several photos of the area, especially the top of the stairs and the hallway leading to them. Later that evening, after the investigation, we examined the photos. Two of the shots showed a patch of blue on the floor, but the patch moved along the floor from one shot to the next, toward Susie. The patches had not been visible by sight when we were standing in the hallway.

As I mentioned at the beginning of this chapter, as paranormal investigators, we never think about the events we encounter as having anything to do with us personally, and at first we didn't attach any special significance to the moving blue patch.

Here, however, is the revelation that struck us in the aftermath of the Clark Chateau investigation—one, we told ourselves—that should have been obvious to both Susie and me at the time.

Earlier in the day, while sightseeing, my wife and I had spent time at the Butte copper mines. During that trip, we talked extensively about her first husband, Robert, and the wonderful times they had had on their trip to Butte decades earlier. Most people knew her first husband not as Robert but as Bob.

He had passed away over two decades before Susie and I visited the Clark Chateau—from a massive heart attack.

Was that why the EMF meters in the séance room were beeping like a heart monitor?

Another startling revelation that I learned from Susie: as a child, Bob's parents had attempted to force him to learn to play the piano, but he rebelled and refused to do so.

Had he finally fulfilled his parents' wishes in the spirit world? Was that Susie's Bob playing the haunting sonata in the parlor room?

In retrospect, it was as if by talking for hours about Bob's trip with Susie and all her happy memories of that time we had somehow conjured up Bob's spirit. This perhaps was also why the EMF meters worked only on her side on the table, and spoke louder when sitting on her lap.

As for the blue patch: a month or so later, while looking at the photos Susie had taken, her sister Georgia mentioned that Bob had been buried in blue, his favorite color.

Can a spirit actually return to those they love when their name and happy memories are evoked?

Why not?

I've always felt that my Grandpap is with me at all times, like an angel perched on my shoulder, ready to protect me.

This was an unforgettable ghost hunt, in the end proving, perhaps, that love truly never dies.

—CHAPTER 11—

Invitation to a Ghost Town

As mentioned in an earlier chapter, I regularly tour with my hypnosis and magic shows in the Rocky Mountain area during the summertime. I had a week off from touring in the summer of 2021, so I decided to take a deep dive into a serious ghost hunt. Rather than my wife and I traveling to a "haunted location," I decided to contact my friend Elies Adams of the Bozeman Paranormal group. Elies is literally the go-to person when it comes to ghost hunting in Montana. She has spent years collecting evidence at supernatural hot spots throughout the state. On this occasion, Elies invited us to join her and her group on a journey to what she considers the most active haunted location in all of Montana, the Old West town of Bannack. For me the thought of hunting ghosts in a legitimate ghost town was intriguing. Although I had visited several so-called ghost towns as a tourist through the years, I had never conducted a serious investigation of one.

What made this hunt a bit unusual was that we had to do it in the daytime. Bannack is now a state park, and although it has hosted a few official nighttime ghost hunts, our access would be limited to the day, along with that of other tourists.

I've always believed that being surrounded by serious participants at night, especially during the witching hour of 3:00 a.m., was the most effective way to investigate and gather solid evidence.

This adventure would prove that concept wrong.

As things turned out, this investigation would result in one of the most terrifying events I have ever encountered. Bannack, I discovered through my research, was founded in 1862 and named after the local Bannock Indians; somehow the town's name was misspelled, swapping the O for an A. Exponential growth followed the discovery of gold in 1862. Amazingly, the last full-time residents left in the 1970s, but at its peak Bannack had a population of about ten thousand. Bannack was, during the1860s , extremely remote, connected to the rest of the world only by the Montana Trail. Even though remote, Bannack briefly served as the capital of the Montana Territory in 1864 and was its center of commerce. In its heyday, the town boasted three hotels, three bakeries, three blacksmith shops, two stables, two meat markets, a grocery store, a restaurant, a brewery, a billiard hall, and four saloons. All the buildings were constructed with logs, and since it is now a state park, they have been maintained to appear as they were decades before. Even today, when walking down the street, you will see faux decorative storefronts, just like in the Old West towns on TV and the movies.

Mining in Montana was grueling work. Though it is a state filled with natural beauty, the weather can be extreme. Typically there are no more than three months of summer, sometimes less. Fall is brief, winter unforgiving. Many miners didn't survive the brutal cold, and even those who did would sometimes go home empty-handed.

Modern ghost towns that once flourished thanks to the gold rush have histories drench in murder, disease, greed, corruption, gambling, and promiscuity. Bannack was a colorful but corrupt town laced with the evil that has plagued men's souls from the beginning of time.

My imagination brimmed with the possibilities of what might happen during our investigation there. I have learned that when sudden, violent deaths occur, and unfinished business remains upon the person's passing, it's reasonable to expect an uptick in spirit activity. Bannack was a perfect storm of sudden, violent deaths. But would those spirits feel comfortable enough to present themselves during the day? And would they manifest while casual tourists were unintentionally disrespecting what were once their homes and places of business?

We could only hope.

After pulling into the parking lot, Susie and I walked down the dirt and gravel road toward the entrance of the town, where we were greeted by Elies, who had arrived shortly before us with her team, which included two other paranormal investigators, Cindy and Joshua. Although most of my hunts are solitary affairs or with Susie, I am always happy to have additional trained investigators along for the ride, especially on hunts that involve multiple buildings and hot spots.

Despite having been abandoned by full-time residents, Bannack remains well preserved and mostly intact, with over twenty-five buildings to explore. It is a living museum of a time long past. I could easily imagine the people who lived here long before stepping out of buildings to greet us. I decided to start my investigation on a hill above the town, at the location where gallows had once existed. In more recent times, artisans had faithfully re-created a facsimile of the original gallows, which had fallen apart over time.

As I stood on the wooden stump that was necessary for the convicted criminal's neck to reach the hangman's noose, emotions overwhelmed me. Standing in that spot, where so much trauma had occurred, jump-started my sixth sense. I was primed to communicate with the other world.

When we returned to the main street, the first building Elies took us to was the old Methodist church. While it may seem to some that a church would be the least likely spot to encounter ghosts, quite often the exact opposite is true. To the living, a church is a place of comfort; why wouldn't the dead find it so as well?

The church was, for the most part, intact, complete with pews and the minister's podium and lectern. Here is where I began to realize that Joshua had special abilities that no other member of our team possessed. Being deaf, he uses his other, heightened senses to organically feel the presence of spirits. Through the soles of his feet he can feel subtle vibrations that the rest of us require equipment to discover. Joshua also can sense changes in the atmosphere of a room that are undetectable to the rest of us before our devices register them.

Elies placed her EMF detector on the podium floor; I placed my iPad, with the Sono X ghost box app engaged, on the minister's lectern; and Joshua placed some motion-activated balls (cat toys) in an empty parishioner's seat. Joshua's cat toys were something new to me. I found it fascinating that a simple cat toy might be a useful tool in ghost hunting, but we would soon find out they were just that.

We were all working in concert, as a team, to make contact with any spirit or spirits who might be present. We were not calling out to any specific minister, because throughout the history of Bannack, due largely to its remote location, the pulpit was regularly filled with "circuit riders" and a rotating cast of clergymen. Could some ghostly minister still be leading a service for his spectral parishioners? We began to call out to anyone who wanted to communicate. Although it was a reasonably warm day outside and daylight poured in through the large windows, the church itself seemed to rapidly get very cold. As we continued to call out to the beyond, Elies's EMF detector began to pulsate and beep, and we all quickly approached the device for closer examination. While the detector pulsed, I walked over to the minister's lectern and called out. In just minutes, my ghost box became alive, which was promising, but what happened next was downright spooky:

"Mezmer," the box said.

Not once, but again and again.

Remember, the Sono X app works by verbally rotating a bank of random words and phrases, and when spirits wish to communicate, they select and manipulate those banked utterances into meaningful phrases to make their presence known. One thing that is not in the bank is anyone's personal name or information, so when the device started saying my name—not once but several times—we were, to put it mildly—shaken.

When the device started saying my name—Mezmer—not once but several times, things became shockingly real to all of us in the building.

Even Elies, a very experienced paranormal investigator, was a bit startled. I heard Joshua beckon me over, obviously excited. He was pointing to one of his cat toys sitting on a church pew. As I approached the pew, I was blown away: not only was it chattering away, but many of its lights were flashing. The room felt aswirl in spirit activity.

Sadly, a group of tourists picked just that minute to enter the church. Talk about bad timing! Once spirits are distracted, it is very difficult—if not impossible—to reestablish contact; faced with no choice, we opted to move on to another building.

After briefly stopping at the attic of a house, where we experienced some interesting, though not particularly dramatic, spiritual activity, we moved on to the jail and the larger holding cell adjacent to it. Interestingly enough, at the peak of the gold rush, the jail was rarely used, as those who broke the law were warned, banished, or hanged. Joshua indicated to us that his camera was flickering off and on for no discernible reason; of course, it is well-documented by generations of ghost hunters that any electrical device can be strangely affected when intersecting with spirit energy, but no matter how many times it occurs, the phenomenon is still surprising, at least to me.

Nothing else measurable on our devices happened while we were in the jail, so we moved over to the holding cell, a claustrophobic space that once upon a time had housed doomed men. This was a dark energy that was very different from what we had experienced in the Methodist church. Chains and shackles were attached to the floor and ceiling, and the cells were designed so that longer chains could run through them, allowing multiple prisoners to be shackled together. The main window looked toward the hill where the gallows stood, so the prisoners could see what awaited them. It is no wonder that we all were experiencing a sense of heaviness, and a dark energy seemed to engulf the room.

A bit of important history: in the 1860s, Bannack Sheriff Henry Plummer was accused of secretly leading a ruthless band of road agents. People claimed this gang was responsible for a multitude of murders in the Bannack gold fields and along the trails to Salt Lake City. Although some historians have more recently questioned the veracity of these accusations, Plummer and two compatriots, both deputies, were hanged, without trial, in Bannack on January 10, 1864. A number of Plummer's other associates were lynched, and others were banished and threatened with death if they ever returned. Twenty-two individuals were accused, informally tried, and hanged by the Vigilance Committee of Bannack.

Although we were simply sharing stories about the town's history, none of us realized just how powerful the dark energy in the jail, especially the specter of Henry Plummer, would affect our investigation later in the day. It would be the ghost of Plummer who would ultimately provide us with one of the most dramatic pieces of spirit evidence caught on camera that I have ever documented.

We moved on to the schoolhouse and, upon entering, once again sensed a wave of spirit energy. It was filled with old desks, and on the blackboards were written school rules and teacher guidelines from all those decades ago. It was as if nothing had been touched in all those years, and any minute a teacher might be ringing the bell beckoning students to class.

Joshua shared that the last time he had investigated the schoolhouse, a small door behind the desks had flipped open. Once again we all started reaching out to any spirits that were present. As I mentioned in other chapters, my way of communicating verbally with spirits is a bit different from those of others in our field; I use the same "lullaby phrasing" that I employ in my hypnosis work to reach the spirits. I find that lullaby phrasing often creates an emotional bridge to the spirits.

Our electrical-based equipment was proving ineffective in the schoolhouse, so Elies and Susie decided to pull out dowsing rods instead—an organic method of spirit detection. Generally speaking, rods, unlike the more sophisticated devices we use, do not provide definitive evidence, but for certain situations they can be more sensitive.

"There seems to be a presence here near this desk and the blackboard," Susie said.

Elies and I, each working independently, were led by our rods to the specific spot in front of the classroom that Susie had indicated. We decided to position ourselves at different ends of the classroom to see if we once again were led to the same spot, which we were. Elies placed her meter on a student desk at the hot spot in the front of the classroom as a spirit anchor. We were unsure if our rods were responding to a spectral student sitting at a desk or a teacher standing at the front of the room.

We decided to separate again, moving on to other points in the classroom, led by our rods, but this time to attempt to physically resist going where they wanted to lead us. As the rods began to lead us to the same spot, I literally tried to physically point them and walk in a different direction. The rods would not allow it! It was like a ghostly hand was grabbing hold of the ends of the rods and pulling me where it wanted me to go. I could not resist, no matter how hard I tried, and the same was true for Elies. I think that had I resisted any harder, the rods would have literally flown out of my hands in the direction they wanted to go!

This time, when Elise and I reached the spot in the front of the classroom, a family with children entered the building. Just as had happened earlier in the Methodist church, the spirit energy dissipated almost instantly.

After examining the video evidence, I felt it was more than likely that it was the teacher's energy that was drawing us, as it was strongest in front of the blackboard.

Next up: the old county courthouse, which in later years would become the Hotel Meade. I was beginning to get the feeling that with each successive building we visited, the spirits were becoming more accepting of us, perhaps even following us from building to building and alerting their spectral neighbors of our presence and perceived intentions.

Upon entering the Hotel Meade, we began by splitting off into groups and conducting independent investigations. It quickly became clear that the hotel was in fact a hot spot of activity.

Susie and I headed up to the second floor, where her EMF meter began registering a high response. Joshua also sensed activity there. We all met up in what had probably been the original dining room of the hotel, where Elies shared a story about a little girl named Dorothy who had lived in the hotel at one time and drowned in the town's river. Since then, her ghostly apparition had been spotted many times strolling the hallways.

I had placed a flashlight on a table in the room, and as Elies was telling her story, some tourists with children walked into the room. As the children passed the table, the flashlight first turned on, then became even brighter. Unlike earlier in the day, when tourists entering our space had seemed to halt our sessions, this time the presence of the little girls seemed to enhance spirit activity. We suspected Dorothy was happy to see children her own age and wanted to play with them. Even more interesting: after the girls left, the flashlight first dimmed, and then went dark. I can tell you that experiencing this type of phenomena in person is a chilling experience you will never forget.

After Dorothy appeared to leave the room, or simply decided to cease communication, we decided to leave the Meade. On the way out, for some inexplicable reason, Cindy's camera went completely dead. She had just put a fully charged battery inside, and yet, within seconds, the battery was completely drained of all power.

I am always curious why batteries often get drained in paranormal situations. Is it that spirits are absorbing the energy for their needs? Are they trying to communicate with us by demonstrating their presence?

It is a mystery that probably will never be solved—at least until we reach the other side, that is.

Our final stop of the day would also prove to be our darkest.

Elies took us next to Skinner's Saloon, which was originally located in Yankee Flatts, before Skinner, who had spent time in San Quentin Penitentiary with his friend, former Bannack Sheriff Henry Plummer, moved it to Bannack. Plummer, along with his corrupt road agents, spent a lot of time in the saloon, so in many ways it was the center of corruption in the town. We placed our devices throughout the saloon, and as usual, Susie was videotaping the investigation. Hesitantly, I decided to call out for the spirit of the infamous Henry Plummer, at which point we noticed a change in the temperature of the room, which became significantly cooler. It was then that Joshua began having a strange paranormal experience.

As he beckoned me over to where he was standing, near the old saloon piano, I could see he had a look of concern on his face. Elies interpreted for me: Joshua was feeling the old wooden boards of the floor move and pulsate under his feet, as if they were alive.

What happened next was beyond my expectations, and is the type of phenomenon rarely genuinely captured on camera: the presence of a classic poltergeist. Fortunately, we had two cameras running, one handheld and one stationary. Even luckier, the stationary camera was pointed exactly where it needed to be, at the front entrance to the saloon.

As I continued beckoning the spirit of Henry Plummer, I casually walked across the creaking floor of the saloon, passing by the old barber's chair in the corner of the room and the player piano. I then turned toward the bar and the back of the room, keeping an eye on the large mirror behind the bar, as sometimes mirrors exhibit strange properties. Next I turned toward the front of the saloon and started walking over to the entrance door. I had shut the door completely, engaging the latch mechanism into the strike plate, so it was closed and securely in place. As I continued calling Plummer's name and neared the center of the room, I felt as if a psychic electrical bolt hit the room; the front door not only opened, but slammed violently against the inside of the frame.

Henry Plummer was angry, and wanted us to know it.

My adrenaline level jumped sky-high.

"Did you see that? Did you see that?" I shouted to Susie.

Susie did not have her camera aimed at the door, but fortunately, Elies's stationary camera caught the amazing sight. Understand there was no real wind to speak of that day, just a gentle breeze, but certainly nothing that would have caused the heavy wood-and-lead door to swing open with such force.

The word "poltergeist," translated literally from German, means knocking or noisy spirit. At the end of the day, we had found a malevolent, violent spirit still intent on demonstrating that he was in control of the town.

—CHAPTER 12—

Call of the Voodoo Drums

I have saved what I feel to be one of my most unusual ghost hunts for this final chapter; it is a brief story, but nevertheless a fascinating one. This final story is a bit different from all of the others in the book, as it involves an investigation conducted under a privacy agreement. I had never done this type of ghost hunt before. I had performed private magic and hypnosis shows for the well-to-do in Beverly Hills with elite clientele who insisted on anonymity, but my supernatural investigations had always been videotaped and available to the public. In any case, in this story I will not be able to share the actual names of the people involved or the specific location where it happened, so we will name my client Tony and his daughter Dawn.

I actually was asked to conduct this hunt after one of my shows. During my performances I regularly mention that I am a ghost hunter, and in this case an audience member came up to me afterward.

"Hi, my name is Tony, and I have been having some strange things happening in my house," he confided.

"What kinds of strange things?"

"I'm a musician, and when I am recording in my home studio, things move for no apparent reason, and sounds are found on our recordings that came out of nowhere."

"What kinds of sounds are you hearing?"

"Very low voices, almost like chanting," he answered.

"If you want some help with it, I'd be happy to come over and check it out," I said, offering him my card.

A few weeks passed and I hadn't heard anything from the man, but then, one day, the phone rang, and there he was on the other end. We set a date for the investigation.

I routinely like to conduct limited research into any location or subject I am about to investigate, but not in-depth. My goal is to get a feel for what I might be walking into. This time, however, I was working with a high-end client, and I knew my time with him and access to his home would be limited to two days. I also knew he expected results. I couldn't find much information on the house itself, so I decided to look into Tony's professional career.

As I suspected, it turned out he was the drummer for a prominent rock band. This revelation provided me with insight that would prove to be important later on in the investigation. I also decided to dig a bit deeper into Tony's family tree and found he was, in part, of Haitian heritage. This too would prove valuable.

In some ways, I felt more prepared for this investigation than any other I had conducted. Of course, it is not always a good idea to be too educated on a subject before an investigation, since you risk forming preconceived ideas. It is better to be led by the spirits and deal with whatever emerges in the moment.

I suspected that Tony's drumming and Haitian ancestry may in some way have been the catalyst for whatever it was that was happening in the house. Having traveled extensively, I knew that in many religious and cultural rituals, drums have been used to summon spirits. My great grandmother Mariah was full Cherokee, so I know that for the Native Americans, the drum carries the heartbeat of Mother Earth and calls the spirits and nations together. Plus, having visited Haiti on multiple occasions, I knew it was the epicenter of voodoo. Voodoo drumming rituals call upon ancestral spirits, called loa, or lwa, for their aid, instruction, and special powers as the embodiment of certain principles or characteristics. This is vastly different from the black magic, witch doctors, pins in dolls, and zombies portrayed by popular media as New Orleans-style voodoo. So, with this research in hand, I felt prepared to give the best possible effort that I could in the limited time I had for this investigation.

As a side note, I was a drummer during my years in military school and at one point was awarded the John Philip Sousa Award for drumming, so I was also excited to spend time with Tony and talk with him about drumming. I was not surprised to discover that he lived in a gated mansion in Pacific Palisades, an elite section in the Los Angeles area. The driveway seemed to stretch for several blocks, and the house itself, with its tall white columns, resembled a Southern plantation manor. An Aston Martin and Rolls-Royce were parked in the driveway.

Inside the house, Tony introduced me to his daughter, Dawn. I was surprised a girl her age would be up this time of night. I had requested we start the investigation at midnight, when the spirits were busier.

"How old is Dawn?" I asked.

"She's nine, but it's summer, so she loves to stay up and listen to me record."

"Has she been experiencing the activity also?"

"Yes," he said. "That's why she wanted to be part of the investigation tonight."

I am usually hesitant to include children in any investigation; however, my own children, Wesley and Ilia, also grew up in show business and were like little adults from a very young age, so I understood.

This investigation posed several specific challenges: first, the house was huge, and I was working solo. Also, Tony had told me the spirits were acting up during the recording sessions, so I decided to focus solely on the recording studio. Thus, I had to accept that there would be electrical equipment in the room, limiting the types of devices I could use, since EMF meters would pick up false readings. Plus other guests were in the house, so I had to request that everyone not involved in the investigation stay out of the east wing, where the studio was located.

I hoped to get some evidence that first evening, but literally had no idea what I would experience.

I requested Tony and his daughter stay away from the studio that first night. I also asked that the studio be in full darkness, with all electrical devices switched off. As I walked into the studio, I used my flashlight to see where I was going. I decided that for this night, I would conduct a question-and-answer session and hope to make a connection that way.

For the first thirty minutes or so, as I was sitting on a couch in the corner of the studio, nothing happened. Then I thought about Tony and his drumming and decided to move from the couch to the drum stool. I thought by being on the stool, I might make the same spirit connection Tony had.

At 1:28 a.m, the spirits finally began to stir. I started to feel closed in, claustrophobic.

"Are you here?" I called out. "Do you want to communicate?"

Ten to fifteen minutes passed, without activity.

Then, that familiar heavy feeling started to push against me psychologically. For at least twenty more minutes I beckoned the spirits to talk to me, chanting over and over in my lullaby phrasing, "If you are here, let me know."

Then my ghost box got chatty, but in a foreign language, which was especially bizarre because my Sono X's bank included only English words. I recognized it as Creole, the language of Haiti.

Three times I heard the words *"mwen la,"* followed each time by *"sispann rele m,"* spoken in a low, trembling voice that would have unsettled even the most experienced ghost hunter. I had no idea what the words meant at that moment, but later they would become critical to the investigation.

Next, a couple of red lights—small LEDs on a piece of equipment—switched on. The ghost box reverted to random words, and the heaviness lifted. By this point, I was emotionally drained; I decided to head downstairs, analyze everything that had just happened, and share the information with Tony and Dawn.

As I went down the grand staircase, I could hear talking coming from the back of the house, which I followed into the kitchen. Tony and Dawn were sitting at the table eating ice cream.

I filled Tony in and told him I would need to do some further research into the words I had heard on my ghost box. It was late and I was emotionally spent, so I told him I was going to head home and return the following night.

By the time I reached home, the sun was rising, and I quickly fell asleep.

A few hours later, I started to look up the words I had heard on the ghost box, which I had jotted down, spelling them phonetically. When I asked Siri what the first set of words meant, she replied, "I am here."

I then asked the same question about the second set of words.

"Stop calling me," Siri replied.

What a revelation these sentences were. First, the spirit was present in the recording studio; second, it was somehow being beckoned by Tony or his music and wanted to be left alone.

Having discovered this information, I could hardly wait to return to the mansion and move the investigation forward.

"What have you found out?" Tony asked me later that night when I had returned to the house.

When I filled him in, he said, "What do you think that means? What does that have to do with me?"

"Well, '*mwen la*,' or 'I am here,' might have been a reply to me calling out to the spirit," I said, "but I'm not really sure why the ghost would have been angrily telling me '*sispann rele m*,' or 'stop calling me.'"

"What should we do now?" Tony asked.

"We're heading toward the witching hour, so I think it would be a good time for you and Dawn to join me in the studio."

Tony agreed, and the three of us headed to the studio.

In the light, I looked at the equipment with the red lights that had turned on the night before, but were off now.

"What kind of machine is that?" I asked.

"It's a digital recorder," Tony said.

"What do those two lights indicate?"

"They tell me that it's ready to play back."

I was starting to piece this puzzle together: the spirit wanted the music to either play again—or to be shut off. But which? And what music?

"Can you remember what song you were working on when the poltergeist phenomena happened?" I asked Tony.

"I can do better than that," he said. "Let me play you the tracks from that evening, the ones with the voices I was telling you about."

It didn't take Tony long to locate the tracks from that night. He pushed a button, and the red lights that had popped on the night before once again lit up. He pushed another button, and the tracks began to play. It was Tony playing the drum track, and at one point I could almost, but not quite, hear the voices Tony had told me about.

"Is there some way you can isolate the voice a little more?" I asked.

He started pushing some buttons on the mixer board, and over the studio speakers came what seemed to be the same low, trembling voice I had heard the night before on my Sono X, but still covered by the drums and difficult to understand. As we listened, the drumbeat got more intense; once again, the heaviness began to weigh me down.

"Is there anything significant I should know about this track?" I asked.

"It's based on a kind of tribal beat, something new for me and the band."

Just then, Dawn let out a high-pitched scream and fell over on her side. Tony jumped up to help her, but because I was closer, I reached her first and helped her to her feet.

"How did you fall?" I asked.

In a fearful voice, Dawn replied, "It felt like I was pushed by the wind."

I had experienced enough through the years to know what that meant. The drumbeat was angering the spirit, and its energy had knocked Dawn over.

It was about to get even weirder.

The ride cymbal flew away from the drum kit sitting in the middle of the room, crashing against the wall of the studio.

Quickly, I shouted to Tony, "Shut off the music track and the machine!"

Looking puzzled, Tony said, "Okay, but why?"

"I think I have the answer to solving your ghost issue," I said. "I'll tell you about it in a minute, but for now, shut it off!"

Tony did as instructed; the heaviness lifted.

"Are you two okay?" I asked.

Tony and Dawn both nodded.

We all sat down on a leather couch in the studio, and I started to tell

Tony and Dawn what I felt was happening and why.

"The new drum riff you have been practicing goes beyond just a piece of music," I said. "Tony, have you ever heard about how native drums in various countries are used to reach spirits?"

"Yeah. I've studied a lot about drumming all over the world, but I never really connected with it on that level."

"Did you know that you have Haitian ancestors?" I asked.

"Yes, but that was decades ago. Why?"

"I believe that the drum riff you were working on has its roots in Haitian spirit drums. In some way, perhaps, it came from somewhere in the genetics of your past."

"Why would that matter?" he asked.

"Because it's my belief that the drums are, in some way, summoning a spirit from the other side." I said. "That's why the spirit keeps saying, 'Stop calling me.' To your best recollection, did the ghost activity happen any time other than when you were practicing that riff?"

Tony mulled the question over.

"No," he said, "I don't believe it did."

"I believe if you no longer play that riff and erase the digital recording of it, the spirit activity will end," I told him.

Dawn exclaimed, "That would be great, Daddy!"

Tony sighed, "I loved that riff; I think it would have made a great song, but Dawn's safety is more important. Anyway, it could be bad mojo for the band to use it on a recording."

We said our goodbyes soon after that, and on the ride home I thought to myself that this was perhaps the most definitive and concise work I had ever done as a ghost hunter.

I never heard from Tony again, more than likely because the "Call of the Voodoo Drums" had finally come to an end.

Hopefully, for his sake and for Dawn's, never to return.

—CHAPTER 13—

Not Goodbye, Only So Long

When I started on my journey many years ago to investigate the paranormal, I had no idea where it would lead me. I wanted to believe, but as a magician and hypnotist I also was a bit of a skeptic. I can now say, after everything I have personally experienced, that I'm convinced there is something beyond this world. I do not know exactly what it is, but it is real. The body of evidence I have compiled—and that you have read about in this book—makes a very compelling argument for the existence of spirits and supernatural activity. For me, this brings comfort, knowing that we all may continue past this existence.

I want to reaffirm that all of the stories I have shared with you are very personal to me and have impacted my life and emotions in so many ways. Each of these encounters has become a part of my inner being.

Through the years, I have found that you cannot be involved in hunting spirits without being changed by their stories. Ultimately, becoming intimate with the afterlife changes how you look at life, creating a new perspective on where life begins, and on whether it ever really ends. These experiences have heightened my understanding of the value of life, and how every minute is precious. Yesterday is gone, today is happening now, and tomorrow may never come. As my mom, Freda, always said, "Live every day like it is your last."

As a magician and hypnotist, I have always had questions about the concepts of life and death—sometimes I even challenged death and laughed at it. When I was a young man of eighteen years old, like most young men, I felt indestructible. It was summertime, and the local annual Lions Club Fourth of July fireworks spectacular was two weeks away. I was a naive, up-and-coming magician. I needed publicity. I had always been inspired by Harry Houdini, and so I got an idea to perform an escape from a straitjacket. When I say "escape from a straitjacket," I do not mean standing on the ground. No, this was a fireworks spectacular, so it had to be a spectacular escape. I had contacted Ben Roberts, the Lions Club director, to set up a meeting.

At the meeting, I stood before the board members, and Ben said, "Please explain to my fellow board members what you are proposing to do for our event."

I began, "I will escape from a regulation straitjacket while hanging one hundred feet in the air from a burning rope. All your club will have to do is provide a crane for me."

Ben then asked, "What would be the cost, if any?"

"I know of all the good work you do to help with people's vision and that this is a charity event, so I am volunteering to do it for free."

The board unanimously endorsed my idea.

Here's the thing: I had never even touched a straitjacket before, let alone attempted to escape from one. And when I walked out of the meeting, I had one week to purchase a straitjacket, find a device to attach to the crane to hold my legs, and learn the escape. I immediately drove to Hollywood and purchased a straitjacket. I somehow found some leather cattle hobbles with which to hang myself from the crane, and began practicing, with the assistance of my best friend, Tom Rector, and his brothers, Jimmy and Robert. The only way I could simulate hanging from the crane was to hang from monkey bars at the local grade school.

After less than a week of practice, I was in front of thousands of people in the stadium, being strapped into the straitjacket. I had to escape from the jacket before they would lower me back to the ground; in the meantime, fire was burning through the rope I was hanging from! Ultimately, I successfully made the escape, to the thunderous applause of the thousands seated in the stadium. To this day—many decades later—there are people in that town who remember that night.

I now feel it was only by the grace of God that that night didn't end in tragedy.

I have many times looked back on my career as a performer of dangerous magic and thought about how my life could have ended many times. Perhaps if it had all ended that fateful Fourth of July, my spirit might still be hanging on a ghostly crane, trying to free itself in the middle of the still-standing stadium. Looking back now from the perspective of a ghost hunter, I would think that young man was both fearless and a little crazy. At that time, I truly had no understanding of just how fragile life is, or of the consequences suffered in the afterlife of a sudden and traumatic death.

It's important that you understand that I have always taken my ghost hunting extremely seriously. The supernatural entities I have experienced and the evidence I have uncovered during those years of investigations seem a bit surreal to me even to this day. I can understand that someone casually reading this book might continue to be skeptical, because you have not experienced the spirit realm personally. Even for me, being right there and experiencing ghost hunting firsthand, it feels a little like a dream. As I grow as an expert in the field and develop my skills as a paranormal investigator, I continue to be in search of more challenging and difficult cases to explore. There are so many locations around the world that I would love to hunt. In the 1980s, long before I was a ghost hunter, I performed on the Great Wall of China, which is considered extremely haunted. Someday, I want to return there and travel throughout Asia to investigate.

I am hoping that this book might open your imagination to what may exist just beyond the veil and inspire you to investigate the supernatural in your own way. If you just have a little patience, and listen carefully, the spirits are waiting to make their presence known.

I will not say goodbye, but rather so long. The reason I say so long is because of my grandpap—the one who worked in the coal mines in Bridgeport, Ohio. On the last night that I would ever see him, he was standing on his porch, lighted by the glow of a single bulb.

"We had a great time with you; thanks for everything," I told him.

"It was great having you here," he replied. "I really enjoyed seeing you."

"Goodbye, Grandpap, love you."

"Let's just say so long," he said, and so we did.

I did not understand the significance or the meaning of saying so long instead of goodbye on that night, but I have always said the same when parting from friends and family ever since.

As I mentioned in chapter two, my grandpap was spiritual, and so in writing about him for this book I decided to try to understand why he said that to me. In looking it up in the dictionary, I found that one of the earliest uses of "so long" is found in Walt Whitman's poem about death and leave-taking titled, appropriately enough, So Long! and published in the 1860 edition of *Leaves of Grass*:

> While my pleasure is yet at the full I whisper So long!
> And take the young woman's hand, and the young
> man's hand for the last time.
> Remember my words, I may again return,
> I love you, I depart from materials;
> I am as one disembodied, triumphant, dead.

I believe this means "until we meet again"—conveying the message that somewhere, somehow, they doubtlessly will meet, sooner or later. Grandpap was nearing ninety years old that night. In his wisdom, perhaps he knew that although we would not see him again in this life, we would meet again in the hereafter.

I truly feel Grandpap has been my guardian angel throughout my adult life, ever since he passed away, I know he is always with me. Having learned the meaning and wisdom of what Grandpap said to me, I can't think of any better way to end this book on ghosts than by simply saying "So long!"

—ACKNOWLEDGMENTS—

It has been an amazing journey writing this book—both living the adventures that led to its creation and converting the stories into the written word. Although my name as author is on the cover, the truth is, it truly took a team to make my dream a reality.

First and foremost, I want to give credit and sincere thanks to my wife, fellow ghost hunter, and personal editor, Linda "Susie" Davis. Susie's skills in grammar, punctuation, and sentence structure were invaluable in making this book the very best it could be. She truly is my greatest supporter and friend. Without her love and special talents, this book would have never become a reality.

Next, I want to thank my daughter, Ilia Willison, for inspiring me to become a ghost hunter through her love of Zak Bagans and his *Ghost Adventures* television show. Additionally, Ilia has been a major supporter of this book through her encouragement and confidence in me. I will always be grateful to Ilia for believing in her dad.

I also want to thank my friend, fellow author and talented magician Dawn Morgan, for connecting me with the folks at Fayetteville Mafia Press. Dawn and her partner, Anthony Hernandez of *Anthony the Magic*, are both great friends and supporters.

Another big thank you to the owners of *Scary Monsters Magazine*, Don and Vicki Smeraldi, for all their support for my writing through the years. It was with *SMM* that I began my writing career in earnest. If Don and Vicki hadn't believed in me and published many of my articles, I do not believe this book would ever have happened.

Finally, I want to thank David Bushman and Scott Ryan of Fayetteville Mafia Press for reaching out and asking me to write about my ghostly encounters. David has done an amazing job of editing and shaping the book, using fascinating phrasing and vocabulary. Scott's top-shelf layout skills have made the book visually interesting. I cannot thank them enough for making my dream of writing a book a reality.

—ABOUT THE AUTHOR—

Michael Mezmer is a clinical hypnotherapist and award-winning stage hypnotist and illusionist. He has toured worldwide, appearing before presidents, princesses, generals, and luminaries of the entertainment industry, including Michael Jackson. For his extensive performances for the US military, he received a Commendation Medal from Air Force General Brian Arnold.

Mezmer, who has a degree in psychology from California Coast University, is a writer for publications including the Society of American Magicians's *M-U-M Magazine*; *Genii*, the *Conjurors' Magazine*; and *Scary Monsters Magazine*, for which he was honored as runner-up for the Rondo Award for best writer and best article of the year.

He has been featured on hundreds of TV and radio shows and as a guest lecturer on the subjects of magic, hypnosis, and the supernatural at major universities, including the Claremont Colleges. Currently Michael is a board member of The Society of American Magicians Hall of Fame and Magic Museum.

For the past decade, Mezmer and his wife, Susie, have been exploring the supernatural from the perspective of a hypnotist and magician. He is respected among prestigious paranormal societies as an expert in the field. During his extensive paranormal investigations, he has encountered the unbelievable.

For interviews, show bookings, or hypnotherapy sessions, you can reach Michael at hypnomezmer@hotmail.com.

You can also visit these websites for more information:
www.mezmer.weebly.com
www.dangermagik.weebly.com
www.covidnosis.weebly.com